SGT GREAVES

The
GYM BUSINESS

'**If you're serious** about the Health Club business, Ken's book gives you a lifetime's experience and smorgasbord of ideas that will guide you to success. I thoroughly recommend it.'

Bob Sweeney, *Managing Director*
OLYMPIC FIGURE & FITNESS CLUBS

'**At last** Ken Heathcote has written a book about his long and successful career as owner/director of probably one of the best known and certainly one of the longest running modern Health Studios in Britain.

Ken Heathcote can tell you from personal experience all the many traps you may well fall into. The secret has always been, as with all manner of businesses, carry on where the average person would give up.'

Oscar Heidenstam, *President*
NATIONAL AMATEUR BODYBUILDERS ASSOCIATION

'**An authoritative and comprehensive** view of the Health Club business. Ken Heathcote's hand-on-heart approach makes this book refreshingly unpretentious and honest in every way.'
Jim Teatum, *Marketing Development Director*
REEBOK INTERNATIONAL

The
GYM BUSINESS

Ken Heathcote

DAVID & CHARLES
Newton Abbot London North Pomfret (Vt)

To my wife Brenda, my son Paul,
my daughter Karen and Mother and Dad

British Library Cataloguing in Publication Data

Heathcote, Ken
  The gym business.
  1. Gymnasiums. Management
  I. Title
  796.4'06'9

ISBN 0–7153–9259–X

Phototypeset by
Northern Phototypesetting Co Bolton
and printed in Great Britain
by Redwood Burn Limited Trowbridge Wilts
for David & Charles Publishers plc
Brunel House Newton Abbot Devon

Published in the United States of America
by David & Charles Inc
North Pomfret Vermont 05053 USA

Contents

Foreword *by Bill Pearl* 6

Introduction 7

1 Getting Started 9

2 Marketing and Sales 31

3 Day-to-day Working 47

4 Exercise Programmes 56

5 Nutrition 69

6 Anatomy and Physiology 77

7 Future Trends 86

Appendices:

Further Reading 90

Acknowledgements 90

Manufacturers and Suppliers 91

National Amateur Bodybuilders Association 94

Index 95

Foreword

I felt it would be an easy task to write the foreword to Ken Heathcote's new book, 'The Gym Business', mainly because I am so familiar with Ken as a person and the progress he has made in the gym business over the past twenty years.

It turned out to be not as simple as I imagined. What has continued to get in my way as I start, stop and throw away what I have written is my respect and personal friendship for Ken. I have found it hard to separate this from the professionalism Ken has shown over the years as he has progressed up the ladder of the fitness industry.

Ken has become such a leader through hard work, dedication, honesty and respect for his fellow men. He has devoted the last twenty years of his life to this endeavour.

I remember well taking part in the grand opening of his first gym in Bolton, England in 1967. Ken's small family operation has grown into one of the finest gym facilities in the world. His success has come not from riding fads but from living a life-style of total dedication to this goal.

His success in the gym business has not come easy. He has earned it! He has worked hard and his family has sacrificed a great deal to bring this about.

To help assure his success, Ken has travelled extensively throughout the United States and Europe observing the operation of the most successful gyms. He has taken the best of what he has learned and applied it to his own business. He makes sure he retains the high standards he sets for himself and his business. He is no 'fly by night' or 'fast buck artist'. Ken's philosophy and business practices have made him a lasting part of the community he serves.

This is exactly the type of information to be found in Ken's new book, 'The Gym Business'. It is a sensible approach to the modern-day gym business. It takes you, step by step, through what is involved in setting up and operating a gym that will give you similar returns to those Ken Heathcote has achieved if you are willing to do your part. The book is an accumulation of the best and most up-to-date information available that has assured Ken's success.

I can think of nobody better suited to write such a book. I only wish it had been available in 1953 when I opened my first gym. It would have saved me countless hours of frustration, untold amounts of money and a lot of grey hairs. I can't congratulate Ken enough for his dedication in getting such a book on the market. Still, this is what I have grown to expect from Ken. Regardless, if it is his books, his gym operation, his exercise tapes, his mail order business, his dedication to sharing with the less fortunate or being one of the finest human beings I know . . . it all boils down to being Ken Heathcote. I am proud to call him a personal friend.

Bill Pearl
Author, body-builder and former Mr Universe, Mr America, Mr USA

Introduction

This book is about business, about you, the average person surviving in a jungle of competition and commerce.

Forget the Lee Iacoccas, Robert Maxwells, and John Harvey-Jones of this world. This book is not about becoming a millionaire, owning a yacht or a Ferrari or a villa in the South of France. It is, however, a book about success, survival, passion. It is about the countless thousands of small businesses struggling in their economic battles. It is about commitment, dedication and an overwhelming ambition to be the best. Above all it is about winning.

Our first gym was in our kitchen and then we moved out into a cellar purely for body-building and nothing else – full of weights and a few benches. We now have an excellent facility filling every corner of the 975sq m (10,500sq ft) that we have today. Our success came through always, always trying to be better than everyone else, trying to improve.

The gym business has finally come of age. Health clubs, studios, gymnasiums have now become an integral part of our community and it is not uncommon to look in the telephone book and see half a dozen health clubs listed in the business sections of any average-sized town. This has helped to force up the standard of gyms and their service and to establish what was once considered a hobby into a recognised and accepted business.

There is still, however, an abundance of amateurism allied to the industry. A good 90 per cent of the gyms in this country are run by people who have entered the business due to their hobby interest. Very few of these people have sought professional advice or indeed had any formal training in sales, marketing, advertising or accounts.

The bulk of gym owners come from three areas: the body-builder who has made his/her hobby into a means of making a living; the business man who sees the opportunity of cashing in on a fashionable business; and the college graduate who has gained his/her degree in exercise physiology or similar subject.

The body-builder might have negligible experience or training in business commerce. The business man, however, would have the business experience and possibly a background of training in the field of commerce. The graduate would have all the academic training but very little practical experience in either of the subjects. The purpose of this book is to help bring these areas together.

Twenty years ago the gym business was stagnant and almost non-existent. The gym was just that, a room consisting of some barbells, dumb-bells, benches and a few stands and pulley machines. There was perhaps a changing room and sometimes a shower. The highly sophisticated health clubs of today offer a wide range of facilities and also provide comfort, style, customer care, guidance and an alternative to the stresses and strains of modern society.

One of the pioneers twenty odd years ago was Bob Sweeney, now owner of the largest chain of health clubs in the UK. Bob set standards that are still with us today. He was installing showers when only one in every seven households had

Aesthetically appealing machines and selectorised weights were partly responsible for the growth in the fitness industry over the past twenty-five years

a bath. Bob made wall-to-wall carpeting a standard feature in his gyms when the majority of us were still cleaning the linoleum around our 5×4 pieces of carpet, and his gyms had background music when the rest of us hadn't even thought of it.

These standard fixtures are now established patterns. Trends come and go, fashions come and go. The sauna became one of our facilities and stayed. Squash became popular and is compatible with the health studio as are dance and aerobics. Only time will tell if they remain with us.

When man first stepped on the moon and microchip technology took over we were destined to enter an age of inertia. In the civilised world machines have come to the the forefront. Computers programme our machines and have taken what little physical toil remained from our industries. Man must now seek physical involvement in different ways. The age of leisure is the new age and the gym provides a civilised and controlled means of staying fit, trim and healthy.

We are at the onset of a new and exciting era. Developments in our industry will match the rag trade and motor industry and this technological progress will, in turn, bring an increased responsibility and a demand for professionalism from our workforce. Changing life-styles will increase the importance of health and fitness in our society and health care will become preventative, through regular checks and carefully planned individual exercise prescription, dieting advice and regularly monitored progress. The new exciting challenge is upon us.

I see hope for any enthusiast or anyone ambitious enough to make a living out of our excellent profession. If we can do it, so can you!

1 Getting Started

Profit or Pleasure?

The reasons for entering the health studio or gym business are usually that you are interested in health, like to train and have a background in training and a knowledge of body-building. People might even think that it is an excellent way to combine a living with training. The truth of the matter is exactly the opposite. You cannot be running your gym at the same time as training because when you are running your business you have very little time to train.

I personally have trained before work, sometimes at 5am simply because work constantly infringes on time. My achievements in the running field (ranging from racing in thirty marathons, all in under three hours, to running 559 miles between John O'Groats and Land's End, at one stage averaging over seventy miles a day for six consecutive days) were not acquired because of running a health studio but in spite of it. I consider myself a highly motivated person but even so my business needed a great deal of effort.

Bill Pearl, a great achiever both in business and in the sport of body-building, operates in the same way by doing his training in the early hours of the morning and then switching off completely to start work at 9am and run his longstanding gym business. I remember one occasion, some years ago, when Pearl and I were talking on the porch of his ranch in Talent, Oregon, Pearl said: 'Every single day I have to motivate myself to go out there and do it.'

There are few businesses that are as time consuming as the gym business. Most gyms open twelve hours a day, seven days a week. Even after twenty years we are still trying to squeeze twenty-five hours into every day and eight days into every week. Your clients demand attention for all that time. Remember you are working in what is their leisure time. At 10pm when you are ready to go home, perhaps after fifteen hours at work, they will still want to steal a few more moments of your time and chew the fat. For them it is a few hours a week of refreshing change from the monotony of their lives and an escape from the stresses and strains of work. For you it is keeping your enthusiasm at a pitch saying the same things over and over again as people want to come in and look around the studio. You go through the same routine when instructing a beginner. It will be the first time that he has heard it, but for you it will be your thousandth time of saying it.

Each day it will be necessary for your business to enrol perhaps three members. If you just happen to be training or doing a few bench presses at the time then the day's profits will in all probability walk out of the door. Training demands concentration. Equally so does work. It is impossible to justify doing both at the same time.

If you want to get into the gym business for profit alone you will have to assess the potential very closely. For anyone operating a gym alone or perhaps with one or two staff then it can be an excellent means of making a living but I stress that the very long hours and variety of jobs to be done can be an exhausting

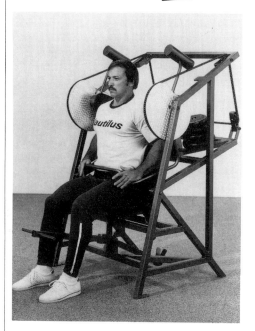 

The start of the boom – one of the first Nautilus machines, the pull-over torso machine – in the early seventies

way of life. Just opening the doors every day, seven days a week, fifty-two weeks a year, can be a mammoth task.

Keeping the gym spotless needs your full attention every day. Sauna baths and shower areas are notoriously subject to infections, even when you employ cleaners. It is a constant effort to keep on top of the situation. In addition, general cleaning duties plus the cleaning and maintenance of the equipment are daily tasks. There is administration work and account books to be kept in order every day. So many things need to be done daily: planning your advertising; filling in your tax returns; VAT; answering telephones; daily sheets; ledgers and invoices. The gym business leaves little time for socialising, particularly when you are doing it all yourself. If, on the other hand, you are to employ people and

consequently reduce your profits, then you will be confronted by a different set of management problems. The choice is yours.

The health club or gym business is not a high profit industry. It is however very much a staff intensive industry. People do need looking after and the more clients you enrol the more staff you need. Failure to provide a proper service can only result in eventual failure.

England is still about ten years behind the commercialisation of the gym business in America. The equipment is similar but we are only just leaving behind the amateur image. We are now experiencing what the American industry has been going through for the past two decades and that is seeing gyms and studios spring up only to go bankrupt at the same rate. The 'get rich quick' syndrome is a myth the Americans know only too well. In a small town the size of Bolton with a population of 260,000, during the past three years we have seen no less than fourteen other gyms set up in competition. It is worth remembering that anything other than total commitment on your part will mean failure.

Raising Capital

Many years ago when we first started in the health club business we had a distinct problem raising money to embark on what most people considered a non-starter. Whoever had heard of anyone making a livelihood out of the gym business, and especially in a town like Bolton?

My first attempt to raise money was met not just with disbelief but almost with ridicule. My bank manager's reaction was in fact that of laughter, almost too funny to discuss. My partner and I, with wounded pride, slunk out of the front door of the bank. Faint hearts however never won anything and our accountants in those days advised us to try their bank. With this encouragement we put a proposal together that was satisfactory both to us and to the bank.

My partner and I had to use our respective houses as collateral. That was fine except for one thing, we didn't own them. The Building Society did. We borrowed from relations so that we could pay off the mortgage, so in effect we borrowed money to borrow money. That satisfied the bank but only to a point. It was my job to do a projection of the proposed costings, turnover and running expenses for the first twelve months of business. How many members? How much would we charge? What would the overheads be? A little bit like running a house? It was the blind leading the blind but the profit predictions came true. The first year's turnover exceeded £30,000, £10,000 more than we had expected.

The last twenty years are now history. From humble beginnings we now have a remarkably well-equipped complex of facilities. We employ over twenty staff and our success is widely accepted and recognised throughout the country.

Before going to the bank you must be well armed with much information on what you genuinely believe your first year's forecast will be: how much you would expect to take in subscriptions, how much you would expect to spend on overheads including rents, rates, heating, lighting and wages. You will have to show a substantial excess of income over outgoings to satisfy the bank. Remember that you have to pay back your loan and the interest it has accumulated. That is your borrowing limit; to exceed it means that your cheques will bounce.

It is imperative to employ a good accountant who will be able to assess the viability of your venture. You, as the ideas man, the entrepreneur, will naturally see the success and all the good things; your accountant will see the pitfalls.

It is also important that you see an early return on your investment, and a predicted cash flow will help to prevent you exceeding your borrowing limit.

Borrowing from the high street finance companies should be avoided, the interest rates can prove to be very high and can be crippling in the early stages.

The economics don't just end at raising the cash. That is, without doubt, merely the start. Sound business sense, hard work, money, time and man management are just a few of the ingredients required for continued success. This is not unique to our industry but is the essence of any business, large or small.

Lee Iacocca, in his autobiography, *Iacocca,* described accountants as 'bean counters'. A friend once said to me that 'they' ask you for your watch and then tell you the time. They can be the most frustrating and practical people you come across. However, sensibility is their forte and their advice and eye for detail should be your guiding light throughout your business life. Dotting the i's and crossing the t's is an exact occupation. A gifted accountant can guide you through the difficult times and help to make the good times better.

Lack of capital is in all probability the reason for most failures in business. You cannot then weather too many major setbacks. Once the business is established, much of the money you take must be ploughed back in the form of reinvestment. This means sinking your profits into other ideas that will hopefully pay off, so that you can make even more money to reinvest into more ideas. Anticipating what the public wants relies on a combination of research and gut feeling. Our first success came with the knowledge that sauna baths were the coming thing. So what little money we had saved was put into the installation of our first sauna. We had immediate success and attracted a much wider range of people. After the second year's business we felt that at last we were starting to learn something. The reinvestment in the form of the sauna had expanded our membership and this policy should be pursued relentlessly.

How and what you spend your money on are vital to your business. Your investment in equipment, for example, could be crucial. The rapidly changing face of our industry means that the lifespan for a good deal of equipment is only about four years. So quickly are the exercise machines changing that new designs and concepts are evolving every few months. The fitness industry is no different from any other business and the hype that surrounds it at the present time is dictating to the gym owners what we should be installing. We are now a fashion-orientated industry and as one

machine comes off the production line a new idea is being put onto the drawing board. Investing in the future can have unpredictable consequences; there is always an element of risk. Your judgement as always is the deciding factor but it would be foolish to ignore popular trends. It is up to you to supply the goods.

One word of warning. With capital in short supply it is often a temptation to cut corners. Always remember the standards you are aiming for and the quality your clients are accustomed to. When setting up or up-dating the fixtures and fittings of your gym try and purchase the best you can possibly afford. Not only will it be a saving in the long term it will also enhance the image of your club.

Location

The first gym that I trained in was an old cinema. The Kings Hall, in those days, was frequented by weight lifters, many of them of great quality. The inside of the Kings Hall was dark and badly lit and equipped with a conglomeration of Olympic bars, globe-type weights and made-up wooden benches. We called it 'the Club'.

The Club was situated near a bus stop and the building had no significance except that it was empty and available. No thought had been given to its position in the town. It was not a business but a room to train in. Inevitably the gym was moved to an old scout hut and from there to a room above a bookmaker's shop, then to a pub and so on.

The present location of the now Bolton Health Studio is just 4.8km (3 miles) from the old Kings Hall. The present building used to house children and was once the annexe to the grammar school. The position is however right in the middle of a large town and thus in a very important catchment area.

Selecting your location is one of the most important decisions of your business life. The business could stand or fall on where it is situated.

Your catchment area is approximately ten minutes drive or a 9.6km (6 miles) radius from the front door of your studio. Calculate the population in that area and statistics show that by charging a reasonable membership fee you could attract 1 per cent of those people.

The amount that you charge has a direct bearing on the number of people you are likely to attract. Charge £50 and you could see yourself achieving a good half of that 1 per cent. Charge £100 and the percentage would be considerably less. It needs little calculation to see that in a town of 10,000 people a professional gym would not survive. The bare minimum in your catchment area should never be less than 80,000 population.

Sustaining a membership to provide you with a living year after year depends almost entirely on that principle.

There are, of course, gyms operating in towns with a population of less than 80,000 but they operate on a very tenuous economic basis.

Your location should be in an area that has a moderate to high income bracket if you are to run a professional establishment. In low income areas you will be forced to charge low membership fees. The size of your community has a direct effect on the size of your membership and equally on the amount that you can charge. Be realistic and assess your competition. Everything in the leisure industry, no matter how big or small, is in competition with you; squash clubs, local leisure centres, small gyms

The layout of Llanishen Leisure Centre, Cardiff, showing the aerobic bank and tummy trim area

and even group classes. However, in spite of all the competition and providing you have the right catchment area, in most cases there will be room for a well-organised and professional set-up.

Take your time in selecting your premises. If they are not in the right area then wait until you can find a spot that is better situated. I would say that 90 per cent of gyms and health clubs are wrongly located and for every one that has a prime spot there are ten that are located in areas that have been dictated by convenience. Even one mile in the wrong direction could make a vast difference to the amount of people you attract.

Town Centre or Outskirts?

Central gyms in towns or cities will always draw from the surrounding areas but if you are on the outskirts then it must be in a high income area and parking facilities become essential. The town centre locations draw shoppers and parking presents less of a problem with most towns these days having ample parking space. Remember, business goes where people go. The more people you have in your catchment area, the more you get into your gym.

Remember that your potential is reduced by your competition. Do your research thoroughly and do not go into an area that is already over-populated with health clubs.

Don't make the mistake of setting up your gym simply because the building is right. Look first at the location and rate this 1 to 10. Here are a few guidelines:

10 out of 10 would have good visibility on a shopping precinct with good parking facilities, or alternatively in a high income area mid-city or high income rural residential area.

7–9 out of 10 – main road, good visibility in a medium to small town, on the outskirts of the town with good parking.

5 out of 10 – little or no visibility from the main road in a low income area with minimum parking but a moderately high volume of people.

Less than 5 out of 10 – don't do it.

Checklist

- Firstly, when choosing your location look first at the population within your catchment area.
- Secondly, look at the income bracket of the people whom you would want to attract.
- Thirdly, find out how good the opposition is.

The Building

If you are fortunate enough to be able to custom build your own premises then the task of layout becomes infinitely easier. Existing premises can have their limitations so it is important that you give layout a lot of thought before you start building walls and erecting partitions.

Individual towns have different restrictions regarding planning permission and I have always found it advantageous to ask the local authorities for their advice, thereby keeping them on my side. This liaison can save you a lot of heartache, money and time and this method may prevent problems arising in the first place.

Work out the size of building needed according to the population in your catchment area. Use the following formula:

Population	Area in sq m (sq ft)
10,000–100,000	930–2800
	(1,000–3,000)
100,000–200,000	1400–3700
	(1,500–4,000)
Over 200,000	1860–9300
	(2,000–10,000)

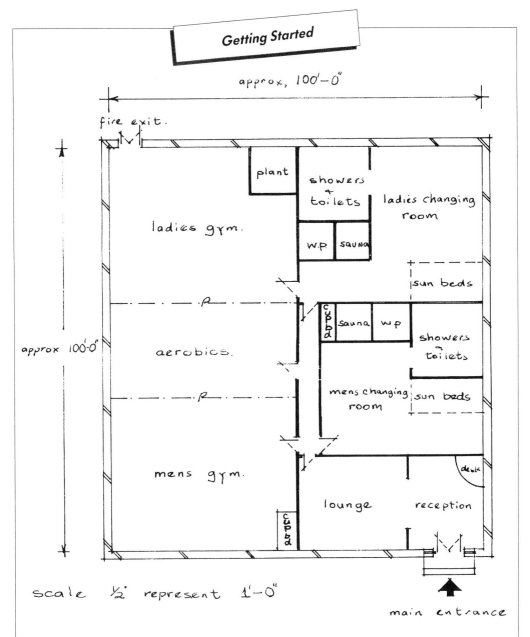

approx, 100'-0"

fire exit.

plant

showers & toilets

ladies changing room

ladies gym.

W.P. | sauna

sun beds

approx 100'-0"

aerobics.

cupbd | sauna | wp

showers toilets

mens changing room | sun beds

mens gym.

desk

cupbd

lounge | reception

scale ½" represent 1'-0"

main entrance

The space needed will vary according to the structure of the building and the type of equipment chosen. Buildings with several storeys are less suitable than those with space all on one level. Ideally all the space should be at ground level; warehouses, filling stations, even old churches can be converted easily into health clubs.

Some years ago, when we first started

Fig 1 A flexible layout for mixed facility accommodation; the dotted lines indicate moveable partitions

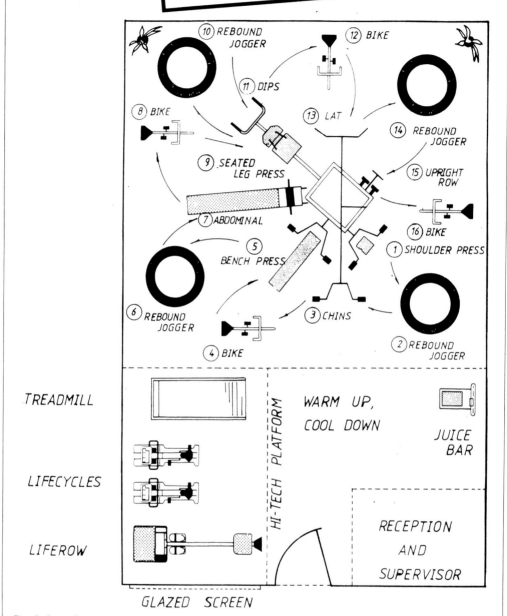

Fig 2 Squash court conversion incorporating multi-station Powerfit circuit and Hi-Tech aerobic platform (*Powersport*)

our studio we had premises that were built into the side of a hill. This caused us immeasurable problems with damp on one wall that went the full length of the building. We were continually painting and no sooner had we painted the wall than a greenish moss would force its way through and then we would have to start

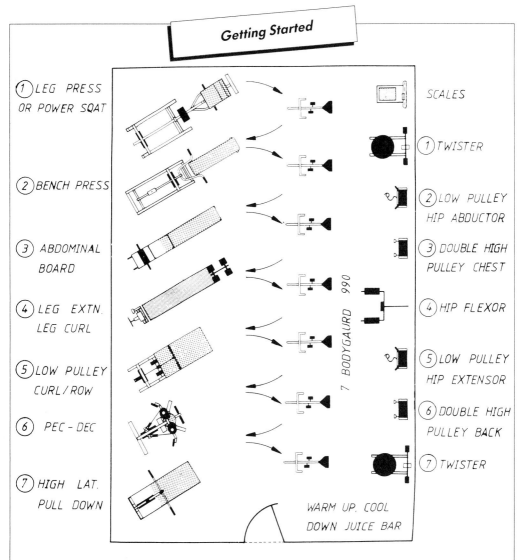

(1) LEG PRESS OR POWER SQAT

(2) BENCH PRESS

(3) ABDOMINAL BOARD

(4) LEG EXTN. LEG CURL

(5) LOW PULLEY CURL/ROW

(6) PEC - DEC

(7) HIGH LAT. PULL DOWN

SCALES

(1) TWISTER

(2) LOW PULLEY HIP ABDUCTOR

(3) DOUBLE HIGH PULLEY CHEST

(4) HIP FLEXOR

(5) LOW PULLEY HIP EXTENSOR

(6) DOUBLE HIGH PULLEY BACK

(7) TWISTER

7 BODYGAURD 990

WARM UP. COOL DOWN JUICE BAR

MENS/LADIES POWERTONE CIRCUIT MACHINES AND BIKES

LADIES POWERTRIM CIRCUIT MACHINES AND BIKES OR REBOUND JOGGERS

again. We eventually compromised and painted the wall green and reduced our expenditure on paint by half.

Whenever possible, and when finance permits, decorate to last. If possible use panelling and mirrors. Even though the initial outlay is high, it will be money well spent.

Plumbing in existing buildings can restrict your layout plans and can be very costly to change. Ideally the building

Fig 3 Squash court conversion incorporating men's and ladies' Powerfit/Powertone circuits and special ladies' Slim'N'Trim circuit (*PowerSport*)

17

should allow you to plan your entrance, gym and shower areas so that they fit in well with each other. You do not, for example, want the changing areas and showers positioned so that customers have to walk through the gym to reach them. If possible try to plan for expansion. Funds will often be limited in the early stages but you may have money available in the future.

When planning the layout of the building the following points are important:

1   Reception is the heart of the studio. It must be visible on entrance to the studio.
2   If possible, have the office adjacent to reception with visibility over the gym. The office must, however, have a measure of privacy for meetings and discussions with staff.
3   Don't skimp on changing space, 60 per cent of your customers will arrive between 6pm and 8pm and so it is important to allocate as much space as you can manage to be able to cope with this busiest time. Similarly allocate as much space as you can for your locker area. Your checking-in system can work well with your allocation of lockers if you oblige people to sign in and at the same time hand in their membership card. They would then receive a locker key for the evening. This ensures that you know who has got the appropriate locker and if they then go home with the key you know who has it. This requires sufficient lockers and space for all your members at peak times.
4   Depending on which type of gym or studio you are offering, you might want to set aside an area for

aerobics or calisthenics classes. If you do not operate an inclusive membership then it is important to consider having separate entrances for both of your facilities.

Most gyms now, even body-building gyms, have floor coverings and many have carpets. Rubber can be very expensive. If you cannot afford carpet then look in the Yellow Pages or classified telephone directory for rubber manufacturers and ask them to cut out 2×1m (6×3ft) pieces to place in front of your mirrors and at the sides of your benches. If you can afford carpets it is still advisable to have these mats to save the wear on the carpets.

The cost of setting up your gym can vary enormously depending on the premises. Weigh up very carefully what is required as regards electrical work and plumbing. Get quotes from different people from each of the trades – three prices for each trade – and also ask for their advice. Consider, very thoroughly the drainage, the tiling of the showers and the ventilation.

With the best will in the world, and even buying second-hand equipment and doing a lot of your own preparation on the building, you will find it hard to budget under £35,000. You must spend a lot of time thinking and writing down your requirements. Do your sums and when you have arrived at a figure, add another 30 per cent – you might then be near to a realistic figure.

Very few people start off with the optimum range of equipment and facilities. Be patient and add to your good quality, basic range as you attract more customers.

Fig 4 In England it is a legal requirement to display a Certificate of Employers' Liability Insurance

Royal
Insurance (U.K.) Ltd.

CERTIFICATE OF
EMPLOYERS' LIABILITY INSURANCE

A COPY OR COPIES OF THIS CERTIFICATE MUST BE DISPLAYED AT EACH PLACE OF BUSINESS AT
WHICH THE POLICY HOLDER EMPLOYS PERSONS COVERED BY THE POLICY

NAME OF POLICY HOLDER

BOLTON HEALTH AND LEISURE LTD T/AS BOLTON HEALTH STUDIOS

DATE OF COMMENCEMENT 01 APR 1988   DATE OF EXPIRY   01 APR 1989
OF INSURANCE   OF INSURANCE

POLICY   05-R5MX14695   REFERENCE NUMBER 165-VB-MH1506 F

We hereby certify that the policy to which this certificate relates satisfies the requirements of the
relevant law applicable in Great Britain Northern Ireland the Isle of Man the Island of Jersey the
Island of Guernsey and the Island of Alderney or to offshore installations in territorial waters
around Great Britain and its Continental Shelf.

AUTHORISED INSURERS
ROYAL INSURANCE (U.K.) LTD

MANAGING DIRECTOR

LONGRIDGE HOUSE
MANCHESTER
M60 4BH

YOUR CERTIFICATE OF EMPLOYERS' LIABILITY
INSURANCE IS ATTACHED ABOVE.

BOLTON HEALTH STUDIOS
30 MAWDSLEY STREET
BOLTON
LANCS
BL1 1LF

Please fold along the perforation and insert the
certificate in the protective cover provided.
A copy of the certificate must be displayed at
all places where you employ persons covered
by the policy. Extra copies of the certificate
will be supplied on request.

003694   R5MX14695-47   (1213)   9700/RNL3F1/1

Mixed Training

In recent years we have seen mixed training in most gyms. There is however good reason for segregation of the sexes and this will depend on your catchment area. The reason is simple; the fastest growing area is leisure for the over-fifties whereas some years ago membership was almost totally from the teenage/early twenties age range. Because of this wide range of age groups, many people feel intimidated – particularly those who are overweight or less mobile – when training beside someone who is younger/fitter/more mobile. This is not so important in some areas where it is possible to have full mixed training facilities, but in provincial towns it is harder to achieve.

Some years ago my partner and I visited New York and we found that most of the gyms were mixed, but wherever possible, some means of division was available. This was at a time when the gyms in America were gaining a reputation for being the singles clubs and particularly the younger age range were training together.

You need to study your clientele before committing yourself to mixed training in England. Certainly in our experience there has always been a larger percentage of males to females in mixed areas. With large training areas you can simply divide your room perhaps with a bank of plants or partition. You can, of course, build the rooms separately, but the main objection to this is the cost.

Insurance

Insurance can be a contentious area and you must be adequately covered. You are required, by law, to effect Public Liability and Employer's Liability insurance and to display the certificate. As government regulations vary, contact a reputable insurance broker who will ensure you are adequately covered.

You must insure the buildings against fire and allied perils and the contents against fire, theft, etc. You may find it difficult to obtain accident insurance within the club itself. The cost can vary enormously and much depends on your claims record. If accidents occur within your premises and it is proved to be the fault of you, your equipment or the immediate environment (carpets, lighting etc) then you are legally liable. It is therefore in your interest to run your club in an orderly way with the utmost emphasis on safety. If accidents occur due to the misuse by clients of your facilities and equipment, no claim can be made against you.

It is virtually impossible to insure against the theft of your clients' personal belongings. You must provide adequate lockers to enable belongings to be locked away and then the onus is passed to your clients.

Always use a reputable insurance company or broker; it may cost you a little more in premiums but their advice and expertise can save you much worry in the long term.

Types of Gym

My definition of a health club or studio is a place where the people who frequent it do so predominantly to work out in the gym, with other amenities being provided. The town or city centre health club can sometimes lean heavily on pretentions and is in effect a golf club without a course but it usually has a pool.

At the opposite end of the scale we have the simple gym which has been with us for many years. These gyms have become popular over recent years because of publicity on TV and cinema. Arnold Schwartzennegar, Nautilus and

women's body-building were the main contributions to their increase in popularity. The *Rocky* films always depicted the trends in training as the macho image continued. It is commonplace now to see body-building books in large numbers in leading book shops. The lean strong look of the female is sought after by model agencies and hardly a day goes by without seeing a World's Gym or Gold's Gym T-shirt worn by passers-by who may not even train.

In simple terms body-building, be it hard core or disguised as just keeping fit, is fashionable and its growth is with us at least into the twenty-first century. To meet this demand the following types of gym have become established:

City Centre/Up Market
Essentially trading to the commercial

The fine lines and aesthetic appeal of David equipment would be wasted in a low-key body-building gym

sector so the clientele is predominantly male. The pool is as important as the gym but it is also necessary to have possibly squash or other ball-type activity. Standards are expected to be very high and abreast of latest developments in equipment. Medically backed advisory service is becoming increasingly apparent.

Rural/Up Market
The emphasis is on country club-type facility. The pool is a necessity and there is no large investment in gym-type equipment. It is important however to have good standards. Marketing to the late twenties/early thirties and upwards

age groups. The lounge areas are important as is a good social atmosphere. A 60:40 ratio women to men.

Town Centre/Slightly Up Market

Marketing to all age groups and having to provide a variety of facilities – sauna, exercise classes, eating facilities and social atmosphere. Working on club-type membership basis, perhaps quarter-, half- and full-year membership fees. High staff employment. A 60:40 ratio women to men.

Suburb

Generally marketing to people who just wish to work out. Usually no frills. Gym, showers, sometimes no saunas. Very often the hard-core type body-building gym. Low overheads and employing a pay-as-you-go basis. Frequented predominantly by the younger age groups and 80:20 ratio men to women or even lower numbers of women.

Fitness Centre

A blend of machines, free weights and computerised running, rowing and climbing machines. The demand is for good standards but providing none of the peripheral amenities such as sauna, pool, relaxation rooms etc. Aerobics would however complement the facility. These are relatively low investment and consequently low risk business ventures.

Selecting the Right Equipment

Equipping the gym is probably more difficult now than at any other time in the history of leisure. New technological developments in recent years have revolutionised gymnasiums and their equipment. Only a few years ago it was a relatively simple job to install a range of dumb-bells and barbells with some benches and pulley machines and little else. Today, and since the invention of single-station cam machines, and of late computer readouts, the needs of the public have dictated constant change and the costs have soared.

At this moment in time we are concerned with the emphasis on machines that are weight stacked, selectorised (see page 00) and where necessary cam-operated. The drift away from free weights in professional gyms and equally the drift towards more cardiovascular equipment in the more up-market gyms and health clubs will continue.

Since the introduction of Nautilus and the increased use of machines, gyms have become much, much safer and far more attractive. The safety aspect has made weight training less formidable and less intimidating to the average person. Nautilus started the ball rolling in the seventies and virtually dictated the trends for some time. But gradually over the past few years other companies have become involved and we now have quite a remarkable choice of equipment in every price range.

The development of cam-operated machines by Universal and Powersport and other companies has helped them equal the Nautilus image. The city gyms operating around the stockbroker belt were expected to provide the best and the named equipment became their hallmarket. Cannons in London was one of the first to see the need for that kind of identification, and installed a full range of Nautilus equipment. However, at the other end of the scale, and almost simultaneously, Gold's Gym opened near Trafalgar Square with free weights being the main attraction and projecting a body-building image. Both gyms had identified their market and were successful.

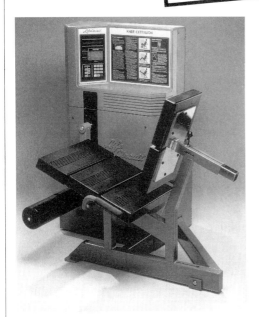

Looking at another market area, Broughton Park Hotel and Leisure Complex has its health club, Drakes, attached to the hotel and serves the up-market rural areas outside Preston. For a relatively cheap installation cost Drakes is now a paying concern. Small in area, Drakes markets specifically to a more affluent clientele and pitches its membership accordingly. The mixture of free weights and machines, good service and low-key personnel projects an atmosphere not influenced by trendy named equipment.

The mixture of free weights and machines can work in almost any area providing there is little or no competition. But this increasingly fashionable industry is beginning to reach even the out-of-the-way areas. As people become aware of the trends, they are demanding more and more sophisticated equipment. With gyms that are similar to Drakes, and there are many like this, the emphasis is on attracting people through the surroundings – hotel, restaurants,

left
Convenience is the key to the Lifecircuit knee extension strength trainer from Life Fitness. Instead of working with heavy metal plates and bars, users simply select the amount of electronically generated resistance from a touch-sensitive console
right
The Lifecircuit arm curl machine works in the same way

pool and bar facilities – so the gym equipment is somewhat less important.

It is impossible to recommend any one manufacturer, there are so many. They do however fall roughly into various categories. Top of the range and approximately in order of price are Nautilus, David, Universal, Powersport, Polaris, Atlanta and Force. If costs are your main concern it is always advisable to have the companies quote on prices. You can always work out a deal that gives you good discounts. Research the equipment. Go into gyms that have been operational for a couple of years and see if the equipment is standing up to the wear and tear. Find out if the back-up

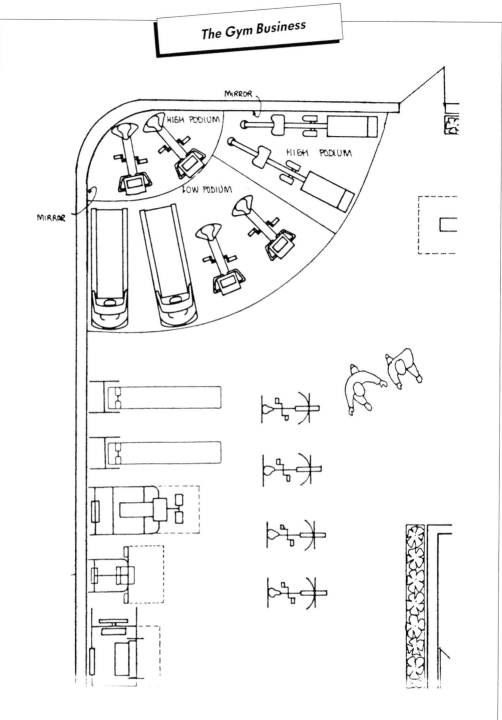

MIRROR

HIGH PODIUM

HIGH PODIUM

LOW PODIUM

MIRROR

Fig 5 Universal's Super Circuit Plan. As an alternative to interspersing your aerobic capacity equipment with your weight-training equipment, an aerobic bank could be installed in one corner as shown here

service is good, bad or indifferent and ask if they are satisfied.

Durability of equipment is as important as its efficiency and its looks. So the gyms with a big throughput should also be on your list. Phone the gym first; I have found that the gym owner is, in general, very helpful and approachable. If necessary shop around for second-hand equipment. With so many clubs insolvent the opportunities frequently present themselves. Don't rush into things, plan carefully. This could be, for the small operator, the biggest single investment and is all-important.

Space will, of course, influence your selection of equipment. If you have a limited floor area then your choice is quite restricted. It then becomes most important that you get the balance right. It is also worth considering having your machines custom made to suit the available space. In the event that your room is an odd shape, then again custom-made machines make life so much easier. The larger companies may have problems supplying what you require so go to a smaller, reliable company. When we equipped our studio, 'Fitness 1', we actually gained enough room to fit in an additional eight stations on our previous gym layout.

The feel of the equipment is also very important as is the aesthetic quality. Remember it is easier to sell memberships if the equipment is easy on the eye when you are taking someone around the studio on a tour. Many people still have a fear of being put through their paces on equipment that they have never seen before. A range of machines, well laid out, greatly enhances the appearance of the gym. If you can stick with one manufacturer this will also help.

The trend in recent years has been to locate the equipment round the outside of your floor space, allowing for circuit-type training. This can however limit the amount and variety of equipment you can house.

Your aerobic machines can be spaced at intervals allowing for the circuit to be used, or grouped into an aerobic bank. Most people start their programme on the bike, jogger or rowing machine. Controlling their use becomes easier if your aerobic machines are grouped together.

When selecting your equipment most of the companies will help out with design and layout advice. If space is limited I would suggest that you perhaps follow the Universal Super Circuit plan (see page 24).

People are impressed with good looking equipment and selected chrome pieces can enrich even the most daunting machines. When Nautilus first came out the essence was on strength, durability (the Nautilus logo was from the sea shell which has survived thousands of years) and lasting qualities. This fitted in with the aggressive age and female body-building came to the fore. This was the time of the macho image, *Dirty Harry*, *Death Wish* and *Rambo*. Things have now become softer, easier on the eye, with more pastel shades influencing the equipment.

We chose Force because we had a say in the size, shape, design and the feel of the equipment. If you are to spend the rest of your working life in the gym the equipment has got to be what you feel comfortable with.

The modern day gyms and studios must be inviting to most age groups and sometimes some of the less attractive equipment can be a little daunting or even intimidating. Multi gyms have never really been successful in modern commercial gyms. The older women, in particular, can be made to feel uncomfortable when face to face with other people when exercising. Most gyms in leisure centres are frequented predominantly by males and usually the younger end of the age range.

As the trends become more fitness-orientated the demand for more aerobic computerised equipment will have to be met. It is important to remember that an individual will spend a minimum of 6 minutes on a bike or running machine and perhaps only 30 seconds on a weight machine – so equip accordingly.

Essential Equipment

If you are limited in the amount of capital investment you can make and your budget only allows the minimum of equipment, or if you are limited in space then I would suggest the following items:

- Shoulder press or 3-way press machine
- Leg-press machine
- High pulley or lat machine
- Bank of sit-up boards
- Low pulley machine
- Thigh-extension machine
- Leg-curl machine
- Pec deck
- Two flat benches
- Twisting machine
- Two or three bicycles
- Motorised treadmill (optional)

Taking this a step further with more capital to invest, the emphasis should be towards more aerobic capacity equipment – with 20–25 stations, 2 running machines, 2 computerised bicycles, 2 standard bicycles and a computer row.

Innovation over the next ten years will include an increase in electronically resisted machines as opposed to weight-resisted machines. There will be an increase in the number of cardiovascular machines with more and more visual displays.

The Pool

A national survey was carried out some years ago in Canada and people who didn't attend health clubs were asked what they considered to be the most desirable facility. Over 80 per cent said a swimming pool.

However, statistics have shown that the least used facility in a health club is the swimming pool. Without doubt a swimming pool is a tremendous attraction to any club and is a very desirable facility. They are also very expensive to install and even more expensive to run and maintain. The choice in the end is yours; your gym and fitness areas will always be busy; your pool, I can almost guarantee, will almost always be quiet.

Sunbeds

Your sunbeds can very often provide your profit margin on your business. Good, well-organised sunbeds are very much an essential to the present-day health club. They must always be kept immaculately clean, in good order and well maintained.

Sunbeds can also be used for special promotions, see page 44.

Setting Up the Body-Building Gym

The gym should be spacious and well equipped with a good selection of machines and free weights. It may be enough for those just starting out to have one machine per body part and the remainder of the gym left to free weights. We are now starting to see many second-hand machines and weights for sale so perhaps you should look at that prospect first. It is amazing what a little paint and plenty of elbow grease will do.

Free Weights

Provide a selection of fixed bars ranging from 14kg (30lb) up to 45kg (100lb) and a range of dumb-bells from 5kg (10lb) up to 45kg (100lb). You will need at least two bench-press bars and one or two squat bars. Reinforce your squat bars by putting a sleeve over the bar. You will also need 136–180kg (300–400lb) for each of the four bars in 23kg (50lb) plates. This could be made up of:

    10×1kg (2.2lb)
    10×2kg (4.5lb)
    20×5kg (11lb)
    20×7.5kg (17lb)
    20×10kg (22lb)
    20×20kg (44lb)
    20×25kg (55lb)

Provide the following benches:

    3 bench-press benches
    1 or 2 incline benches
    1 decline bench
    1 preacher bench

Make allowances in your budget to buy an assortment of occasional bars and incidentals like curling frames. There are so many women now attracted to body-building that it is advisable to have a range of smaller dumb-bells. The important thing is however your *range* of bars and dumb-bells. You will also need collars for each bar for safety reasons.

Machines

The following would give you a sound basis on which to establish your body-building gym:

    Leg-press machine
    Leg-curl machine
    Thigh-extension (knee-extension) machine
    Hack squat
    Calf machine
    Lat pull-down machine
    Floor-pulley row
    Chin bar
    Dipping bar
    Pec deck
    Tricep machine
    Bicep machine
    Smith machine

Body-building gyms will have machines for some time to come with a good percentage of free weights. But body-building gyms are also influenced by fashion so great care must be taken in selecting equipment.

Mirrors are another essential and a good number can be obtained cheaply from High Street shops being refurbished. Very often it is a simple matter of just walking in and approaching the foreman in charge of the alterations and agreeing a price.

The ardent trainer does not require too many additional facilities. One can discount sauna, steam pool, whirlpool etc but a sunbed area with perhaps two beds is desirable. The rest area does not need to be too large; a small juice bar where the guys can chew the fat on completion of their workout is quite sufficient. The changing room, of course, should be adequate. Provide plenty of lockers in this area so that people can secure their belongings whilst training.

Body-building – Responding to Change

It was apparent that the general trend was towards more and more machines with fewer free weights, and gradually over the months we were feeding machines in and filtering the free weights out. At the same time I was taking some

Creating Sandows we lost 60–70 customers overnight and gained 200 in the next year

criticism from the body-builders who thought I was trying to make 'their gym' into a huge multi gym. Body-building was becoming a very special section on its own. The rough and ready element in body-building was breaking away from the industry and was no longer identifying itself with the more sophisticated developments in the fitness industry. The body-builder is a dedicated athlete like a boxer or a wrestler, competitive runner and so on. The body-builders in our studio were in fact intimidating the rest of the clients.

Two things happened that exemplified the need for change. The body-builders moved out and set up their own gym and we lost 60–70 members overnight. We converted the heavy section into an up-market, more sophisticated, gym facility with half free weights and half machines.

The body-builders in their gym had 90 per cent machines and 10 per cent free weights, the very thing they had fought against for so long. We had both responded to change.

Our new converted facility now attracts *all* our clients and is well used by all. Creating a new image and identification by giving the new gym the name of Sandows made the change easier. It generated interest among our members and was something we could use for promotions. The name Sandows originated from the old-time strong man Eugene Sandow who has been called the father of physical culture. It was Sandow who, a hundred years ago, made it quite clear that ladies could benefit from the use of dumb-bells or barbells – weight training. And of course the new Sandows was to cater for both men and women; an appropriate name chosen from the past to project us into the future.

Pitching Your Price

Pricing your membership fees depends first on the depth of your catchment area, secondly on the ratio of professional people to the lower paid and thirdly on who you are trying to attract. Ask yourself who is going to use the gym, how much they can afford, why they should come to you in preference to other establishments and what you need to do to enrol them as members.

In deciding your location, you should have already considered the income bracket of the population. Tailor your facility to suit the area and try to be better and more attractive than your immediate competitors. This will give you an indication of how much you can charge. If you were to ask the average person in the street what they thought the most important thing in life was, most would say 'health'. In reality less is spent on health than on almost anything, and the average health club fee comes way down the list after cars, holidays, TV, videos, clothing, records, smoking and drinking. The money we spend on ourselves and our health is only a small percentage of our disposable income. Membership fees have to be attractive to your market place, realistic in relation to your competition and value for money.

In a town that has a population of less than 90,000, I would recommend a basic membership fee and a pay-as-you-go system. Your level of income will be relatively low and range of expansion minimal. If this sounds negative then it is a hard fact of life. Only the up-market, high income, affluent areas can sustain a professional health club and then it is necessary that the gym is part of a complex – hotel, country club, leisure centre or health farm.

In an area with a population in excess of 100,000, look at the ratio of professional people to factory workers. Do some homework on how much the average wage is. Take into consideration the unemployment figures. In some areas a population of 200,000 would not sustain a good health club charging fees of say £150 per year because of this factor.

In an area with a population of 200,000, with a reasonable percentage in the higher income bracket, not too much competition and with low unemployment, one can perhaps ask a little more than £150. It is infinitely better to start a little high and allow for offers for group, family and corporate memberships. The slightly higher income areas will stand a slightly higher fee but in nearly every case the clientele of the rural and country-type establishment will demand a pool.

In Central London or New York it is possible to charge £500, £600, £700 and more for membership and even in some of the more affluent rural areas in the north of England you could ask that. However in areas such as small mining towns where there has been redundancy or hard times you would be lucky to get £50, £60 or £70. Face the harsh facts, there are areas that will not support a professional gym at all.

The Launch

Setting up the gym is only the start. In the process of putting the gym together it is easy to fall into the trap of forgetting that you are setting up a business which must earn you a living. Getting off to a good start is vital. How you launch can mean the difference between having a good first year's business, an indifferent one or even a failure.

Launching the body-building gym is little different from launching any other gym. Your target, of course, is the body-builder and your advertisements should make that quite clear. Allow a reasonable amount in your budget – say 2 per cent of your overall figure for the initial launch and the next two to three weeks of advertising. It is false economy not to promote strongly at the beginning. Ring up the local newspapers to see if they would like to come in and run a feature. They will do most of the work on putting together a decent article if you can supply supporting contractors who would be prepared to advertise in the feature. These could include your equipment suppliers, any builders who have been involved, carpet suppliers, shower people, tile suppliers etc. In many cases you may even find that if you get enough to come in on the advertisements you can get your space for a very small amount – or even free.

Put on an offer for your opening day and make sure that your assistants are well versed in the selling presentation. If you are working on an enrolment fee and then a monthly payment, do a 'Once Only Offer' and cut the enrolment fee by 50 per cent. Try the discount price on the yearly fee or maybe do a one month opening offer. As an alternative you could do a sunbed offer to anyone who joins on that day.

Have special invitations printed to give to your friends, relations or anyone who you feel may be interested. In fact spread these around. It is important that the gym looks busy on your opening day. This will not be a day for training, so make sure that you and your staff are smartly dressed.

Undoubtedly the best time to launch is in the first three months of the year and the earlier the better. It is almost suicidal to open in June, July, November or December. Plan your opening to suit these early months; they should carry you through the summer.

Remember to try and give the best service possible. Keep the machines well maintained and make yourself available for as many hours as possible. This will not only attract new members but it will help create the right image from the start.

2 Marketing and Sales

Many people confuse marketing with selling. However the two are vastly different. Marketing is providing something that the public would desire but will not necessarily buy until they are persuaded. IBM's Vice President F. G. 'Buck' Rogers described the differences when speaking on 'Riding the Winds of Change': selling is nothing more than the act of persuasion; marketing is a more encompassing term, the process by which an organisation relates itself productively, profitably and creatively to its environment. Selling tries to get the customer to have what you have; marketing tries to have what the consumer wants.

Image Building

Marketing is image building, being seen as we want to be seen. It is also picture painting, creating the right response to both you and your product.

There is always a little magic that surrounds the business of health. We buy food and clothes as part of our everyday life-style and the sale of food is an acceptable part of our society, but the image that is created when working with people's bodies conjures up the pleasantries that are not associated with surgeries or hospital wards. We, in the gym business, are looked upon as being the good side of life with good health and an image of smiling goddesses and young men who are athletic, healthy and strong.

In reality it is vastly different, the work is hard and long. Twelve and fourteen hours a day are commonplace. Creating the right image for your company is a twenty-four hours a day job. It does not just include advertising but is essentially everything that you do both inside and outside the studio.

Marketing is about presentation: the layout of your reception area; the attitudes of your staff; how they dress, speak and act to your clients. Marketing is decor and the colour schemes of equipment and even the plant life you use to highlight the studio's facilities. Marketing is how people see you and how you present your image to your market place, the client and prospective customer. Marketing your gym or studio can be done in a number of different ways and you must always, but always play to your strengths. Create an image, perceive what people want and then supply it.

At one stage in the development of our business it was necessary to establish that we were breaking away from our image of just being a gym. The intense competition in the early eighties required certain changes in our marketing policies. Most of what we had done in the past had been allied to improving our facilities and their appearance. This time, however, I changed from track suit and sneakers to suit and tie. I was still, of course, very much involved in the daily running of the gym and taking classes but the subtle change of being seen constantly in suit and tie separated us from the opposition. I had always said that the gym business was indeed a business and with this change I signified that we meant business. Our policy was to attack every aspect of our community and seek members from every area; this flanking movement helped us to penetrate more efficiently into the business sector.

You cannot create an image overnight. Marketing embraces advertising in the press, leaflet drops to selected areas, promotional brochures, direct mail, sponsoring events and making yourself available for charities and public appearances. Everything naturally depends on cost. Flooding the town with leaflets will have a return but you must quantify the success of such a venture. Does the return justify the initial cost?

Marketing is an industry in its own right and every aspect should be explored to find out what would be the most advantageous means of using it. In our case we have always attempted to present an up-market image. I say that with some reservation. Up market in Bolton is not the same as up market in Mayfair. We have created a working-class up-market image. We have said for many years: 'Come to Bolton Health Studio where you can exercise in pleasant luxury surroundings at a price you can afford.' In other words, luxury on the cheap. If we were to do the same exercise in Mayfair we would have done the same presentation but we would not have mentioned the price. It is only to the money conscious that you say they can afford it.

Identifying Your Market

Identify your market place. Identify your customer. Identify your product. Then supply what they want from you be it the swimming pool, aerobics, sunbeds or group classes.

I was recently invited to speak at a young mothers' meeting. I had done some research on the group and had prepared my talk carefully. I arrived at 1.45pm in readiness for the talk at 2pm. On arriving I was asked to wait in a small room until I was called. The organisation was awful and it was nearly 2.30pm before I started my talk. You can imagine my feelings when I was ushered into a room the size of a small classroom with only seven people to address my speech to. To make matters worse each of the women had two or three young children to look after.

The whole place was pandemonium. I vaguely remember my hostess saying: 'I hope you don't mind a little noise', and then she sat me down to face this small semi-circular group of young mothers.

The children were all over the room, in front of me, behind me, sliding down slides, climbing over tables and chairs. The young mothers at times seemed to be listening and at times oblivious to what I was saying, intent on just keeping the children from getting totally out of order. I still remember controlling my panic and resisting the urge to run from this bizarre and bewildering charade. At one stage, because of the activity of the children, one woman directly facing me was knocked backwards off her chair.

The last words my hostess said to me before I left were: 'I hope you will come back to give us another talk.' Three months later, on one of our annual open days four people came and joined our studio as a result of that talk.

Personal Contact

It makes it easier to sell memberships if you have a good facility and a good product. To sell that product you need people. Getting the right blend of staff is absolutely essential. We look at this every single day of our lives. We look at our staff and we weigh up our strengths and weaknesses. We are people people.

We market across the board. We do not just go for the younger element or the older element. We started marketing to older people some two or three years ago and we now have something like 27 per cent older people as part of our membership – a fairly big input into the gym. So we look for staff who can deal with people right across the board, looking for a balance. It was described in Edward de Bono's book, *Tactics: The Art and Science of Success,* as a mosaic. Getting your staff together is like forming a mosaic of people who identify with your customers.

So we have our younger staff who can identify with the kids who come in and we have older instructors who identify with the older element. We also like something that will bridge that gap. In other words what we are trying to get is a blend of staff who will identify with all the customers who come into our health studio and even more so with people we want to bring into the studio. Selecting staff is very important. They not only have to be fit enough to take classes, be reasonably intelligent to enable them to handle memberships, they have got to look good as well, and that is quite a hard formula to find. You should work hard also to gain loyalty from your staff, since that creates a much better atmosphere for your customers.

We all need certain people. We have an advertising man. In fact we have had several over the years. You need somebody who can identify with what you want and the type of ads you want to put out into the market place. So it is essential to get ad people who talk the same language as you to put your advertisements together effectively. This applies to reps too. When I call the rep for the local newspaper, she comes over and she knows that when I ask for a right-hand page I have to have it. She does not pressure me; if I do not want any ads she leaves me alone.

Advertising

Advertising is specifically transmitting a particular message that you wish to bring to the attention of your prospective customers. Advertising is a kind of selling. It is a visual message to induce people to buy.

The message changes very little and should always have, if not in full, an underlying theme of health, fitness, beauty and self-improvement. Like selling, it is not the product that we must advertise but the benefits. If it is a particular machine that you have just installed, then think in terms of what the benefits are, what the clients will derive from using that machine.

When advertising your club as a whole, point out how people would benefit from using your facilities as opposed to those of your competitors. Remember that people are attracted to us in the first place in order to improve themselves physically and mentally, and secondly to escape the rigours or boredom of every-day life. We provide an escape.

Advertising can be very expensive but with thought and careful planning strategically placed small ads on a very regular basis are a great asset to any business and need not be expensive. Finding someone who is on the same wavelength and thinks the same way as you do can take time. Agencies can be expensive but there are also many freelancers. Do not hesitate to change your ad men if their ads are not working for you. Have them draw up three or four small ads that you can exchange from time to time. Providing you can have them well placed in the local newspapers or magazines you will need little else.

Your ads should be kept clear and concise. Your headings in effect should capture the attention immediately and

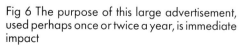

Fig 6 The purpose of this large advertisement, used perhaps once or twice a year, is immediate impact

above
Fig 7 Using testimonials as a means of advertising

your message should be brief and to the point. The textbooks tell us that advertising should be constant to be effective and I have found over the years that this is true. A small ad on a regular basis can be far more productive than a large ad every now and again. It will ring bells in people's minds by constantly keeping your name in front of the public. And so it is not always necessary to spend large amounts of money on advertising. It is said only 50 per cent of advertising works – but which 50 per cent? if you don't promote, a terrible thing can happen – *nothing*. Your methods of advertising or promotion either outside your studio on billboards or posters or in the local newspapers or magazines, are a matter for you to decide – but promote you must.

Advertisements

Because of our reputation and the success of the open days we have run, the words **Open Day** are the eye catcher to this large ad. We are still selling health, fitness and beauty and so our second priority is the 'Top 10 ways to a new you' – announcing the introduction of a new range of classes. The remainder of the ad shows the variety of facilities which we have and our competitors lack. We end by showing the name of the studio, our address and telephone numbers.

It is important that all ads have a 'top and tail'. The top is the eye catcher – the message that you want to get across. The content of the ad should be in the middle and contains the message that you wish to enlarge upon. Your ad must always have your name, address and telephone numbers. The tail could be an offer with a message which says 'Come Down' and a closing date. But the name, address and telephone numbers must be clear.

An effective way of catching attention is to include photographs and brief testimonials from satisfied customers in your advertisements when the people 'speak' the words. Professional layout and design are essential.

Selling

Selling is about two things: asking questions and painting pictures. Did you ever go to the cinema and see a good who-dunnit? The first thing you see is the defence lawyer painting his picture of how the dastardly deed was done. Your mind is taken to the scene of the crime and the cameras show how his client is on the receiving end. The prosecuting lawyer then paints his picture showing the opposite and you are sold first one story and then another. Clever lawyers are good at selling their stories and painting pictures with words. They are also good at asking questions that they already know or think they know the answers to.

There are four kinds of question. Closed questions require only a yes or no and are sometimes called tie-down questions. For example 'Would you be training through the day or in the evening?'. This is to find out if the client would in fact have time to train. Then there is the open question or fact-finding question which usually starts with who, what, where, when or why? 'What is it that you are interested in? Conditioning? Fitness? Body-building?', questions that you perhaps know the answer to but would help you to lead into a question that would in turn lead into a closed question. The directive question can be used if the prospect has perhaps been dissatisfied with a previous club – 'If I could show you how it would be better to train here with us, would that help you to take out a membership with us?' or 'If I could show you that what we have here are facilities and methods that would achieve your desired results, would that help you to decide?'.

The fourth type of question is a reflective question where something was said earlier in the presentation that could help you to close the sale. Most good sales people are good listeners and feed from what the prospect says. The best sales people know when to shut up and say nothing and that is *always* after the question asking if the prospect would like to join. After you have asked this question, the first person to speak loses.

Selling, like any other profession, is an art and needs to be practised daily. Having a good product or service to sell is also important. However, people rarely buy products or services – they buy benefits. Sell the sizzle, not the steak. Sell the hole not the drill. Sell results – a leaner, fitter, more appealing you. Conjure up pictures of how your prospect would like to be and present that picture to him or her. Visualising it for yourself helps enormously in helping to present it to your prospect. But do not make the mistake of talking about yourself. The most important person in the world to you is you. The most important person in the world to your prospect is himself. So the sales person talks about his prospect.

Our statistics show that only about one in ten of the prospects coming through our doors are ready to sign with no further persuasion. This is even taking into consideration that most of our prospects are referrals from our own members and have therefore been part sold on the idea already.

We all at some time hate making decisions. What do I wear today? Shall I wear a white shirt or a blue shirt? My wife went shopping the other day and tried on 34 dresses and then bought the one she had first tried on. How many times have you sat in a restaurant and pondered over the menu, first selecting one dish and then another? I had a friend some years ago who only had one tie. He never had any problems selecting which tie to wear until someone gave him six ties; now every day he has a decision to make.

The prospect is like that. He or she won't have a problem until presented with a possible commitment. 'I just want to look around. Can you give me some details of your club? How much is it to join your health studio? Can I go away and think about it?' In principle everyone who comes in through your front door is interested in joining. And yet barriers to joining are created by them in the first instance. That's human nature. The good sales person knows how to lower those barriers by having good techniques, the right attitude, enthusiasm, body language and of course the right questions and a picture to paint.

Successful selling is an art. Yet the very concept would frighten most people if they had not sold before. Like everything else in life we are governed by the basics. One could argue that good salesmen are born, not made. There are thousands however who are excellent salespeople who have taken it upon themselves to educate and then practise the art of selling.

You must orientate your staff towards selling. To what degree you have them trained is another matter. Often your staff must be able to fulfil a variety of tasks from instructing; cleaning and maintaining the gym equipment; upholding standards and mixing with clientele. Above all, be realistic; expecting your aerobics instructor to take classes, instruct competently in the gym, have the personality to cope with people in every age group, sell memberships and still look like a million dollars, is asking for the impossible.

Selling memberships is little different from selling nuts and bolts, drills, machinery or merchandise of any description. We don't sell the drill, is the old saying, *we sell the hole*. We don't sell the commodity; we sell the *benefits* of that commodity. We don't sell our products, our gym, our superior facilities or our highly trained and qualified staff. We sell the benefits – a better physique, a shaplier figure, better health, a more vibrant you. Everyone wants to look better, feel better, be better. Having a good product, however, helps to paint the picture of the road that leads to achieving the goals people desire.

People are now more educated than at any other time in our history. Trying to

fool people into buying something they know to be shoddy will be fruitless. People now want more than just a place to work out, a sweat box or facilities that are inferior, unclean or manned by uniformed staff who put themselves before their customers. In other words the product has to be good. If the product is good then you are more than half-way to selling the prospective member a membership at your club.

Al Phillips, a Vice-President of the Bally Corporation in Chicago, is emphatic that a good product is vital to success regardless of how good the selling may be. The latest installations at the Health & Tennis Corporation of America bear this out as does the Barbican location in London, one of the most successful branches worldwide.

The image we try to depict – male, female, machine, beauty and aesthetic appeal – our super gym, Fitness 1

The Selling Tour

You need conviction, a positive approach and persistence to assure your

prospective client (or prospect) that she/he wants what you are selling. You will have ample opportunity to put over these qualities whilst conducting a tour of the health club's facilities.

Never short change the customer or prospective customer. When you do the tour, show them everything if necessary. If the customer is ready to join there and then, then of course sign them up there and then. If, on the other hand, they require a specific part of your facilities, then that is what you must concentrate on. Don't for example spend too much time on a facility that they show very little interest in. Get their attention; find out their desire; make every attempt to convince them that you have what they want and take action on that by asking for a close.

Each club, studio, gym or leisure centre is different. But the basic principle of selling remains the same. Remember you are not selling the facilities, you are selling the perceived value of those facilities and the benefits to the customer.

Stanley K. Mann's *Business is Great,* written nearly twenty-five years ago is still a source of sound information, a tribute to his professionalism and his knowlege of the gym business. One of the things that has changed however is the selling technique. Think positively and form a framework for a logical sales procedure. The selling framework comes into three areas:

● Introduction
● Presentation
● Close

Introduction
The introduction is a simple, although very important, part of the sale. There is always a: Hello; smile; and my name is . . .

This is your first moment of contact and it is important that there is no intimidation. Put the prospect at ease. It is also important here that you ask for his/her name and take a few particulars that will help you give a better tour of the studio. Explain what you are doing.

It is always advisable to have a visitor's card. It gives you the opportunity to fill in the card with their name and address. Ask questions with questions: Married? Children? Any past history of exercise? What are you interested in? Losing weight? Keeping fit? Whatever their answer make sure you answer with another question. Show interest. Listen to what they have to say and show you have listened.

Information coming from initial exchanges can be a process of building up a personal profile of the prospect. It also gives you the opportunity of clarifying the time that he/she would want to come to the studio. Would you be able to come in through the day or would it be in the evening? This is a tie-down question that requires one of two answers.

Once you have found out the reason why he/she wants to come to the studio you can then start to sell the benefits. Paint your picture of how you would approach their particular problem. This process should take only two or three minutes and should be carried out a little way from your reception area. Respect their privacy – a small desk partially hidden from reception, not intimidating in any way but private enough not to be interrupted by passing people, is ideal.

During this first introduction you have eliminated the problem of time – one of the biggest objections. You have found out why he/she wishes to exercise and have paved the way for the presentation and the selling of the benefits. The introduction should take no more than five minutes but it is where impressions are made. Above all, you should aim to make your prospect feel at ease.

Presentation

You can now structure your presentation to suit the individual. Make sure that when you are ready to take them on the tour you say that you will be bringing them back to the desk to explain how you will put a programme together. You want to show them how professional you are. Prepare yourself at this stage to sit them down and complete whatever paperwork is required.

The next step is to explain *how* you are going to do it. The conversation should continue and it is here that you are looking for responses.

> Question   Is this the type of facility
> you are looking for?
> Answer   Yes
> Question   Could you see yourself
> using this equipment?

If you have found out enough during the introduction and done your job properly then you can focus on and sell the benefits at this stage. If it is conditioning, go over to the bikes or running machines. You could have a programme ready that shows the results of someone else's success with a similar problem. Throughout the tour use the prospect's name but do not overdo it. Remember that this is also a listening process. The presentation is the most important part of the encounter, you should be drawing out the information and answers you require.

Remember at all times that he/she has *come to you*. There is a desire to work out for any one of a dozen different reasons and it is up to you to kindle that desire. Show them that you are enthusiastic about your club and that you would like

to look after them. Remember that people do not buy on price but on perceived value. If you can show them value the price becomes secondary.

If at any stage they ask for the price tell them the average price per week but it is better to give details at the end of the tour. If you have an offer on at the time, say so and say you are sure that you have a membership to suit them.

During the tour try to create some common ground or a compatibility with the prospect and yourself. The sale is really made during the presentation and the close can be made at anytime during the tour providing you get the right response. It is, however, usually completed at the end of the tour at the point where you started, the desk.

The Close

On returning to the desk, sit your prospect down and explain what you have to offer regarding fees. The fees, of course, are decided by you. If you *do* have an offer this is the time to make your pitch. One method that we have used with a great deal of success is to have your offer on the first visit basis. Explain that your fee is say £150 cash payment, but if they pay *today* there is a reduction of 15 per cent saving them £22.50. You are now moving into a tie-down situation when you can say: 'Alternatively we have very attractive terms – with a deposit of £50 and £x per week or month and if you join today I can reduce your initial deposit to £25. **Which payment would suit you?**' Then you must shut up. Let the prospect decide – the first one to speak usually loses. If they decide to join – fine. You have converted a prospect to a member. If, on the other hand, they say they would like to think it over then you may have lost them, at least for the time being. Agree with them if they seem unsure and ask if they would like to have a free trial workout. Give them a free pass and arrange a time for them to visit you again and hope that you have another opportunity to convert them to membership. At no time must you come on too strong – in the long term you will only diminish your reputation. At all times think positively that you are going to help the next prospect to convert to membership.

There are many different types of sales presentation and being successful can depend on a number of different things but it is human nature to go for a bargain. One technique that has worked for us for many years has been our open day when it has been widely recognised that there will be an offer available. Naturally we can't have an open day every day of the year but you *can* have an offer for first-time visitors. During the presentation the offer can be mentioned and on sitting them down at the end of your tour your close can be administered then by telling the prospect that this offer can only be available on this first visit.

The offer can be a 10 per cent reduction, a reduction in monthly fees or enrolment fees or whatever you feel is an honest, attractive, viable offer. If the prospect does not want to take advantage of the offer, make it clear that on returning another day the full price would have to be paid and stick to that. Having an offer or an attractive payment plan, weekly or monthly, makes it easier to ask for the close – but ask you must.

Only practice and persistence will give you polish on your sales presentation. Remember you will say the same thing time and time again but for the prospect it will be the first time he or she has ever heard what you have to say.

Many clubs create a waiting list either by design or simply because they are full. The procedure of the tour is the same. You must never tell your prospect that you are full until you have given them the tour and the presentation and sold them the benefits. Even when you are full you still require a waiting list; you still have to sell your product; you still have to paint your pictures. You have, in the end, to close your sale by telling the prospect that he cannot join thus creating a greater desire to join. We all want the unobtainable!

Naturally there are not many people who are in the fortunate position of balancing the income and number of members to keep the happy medium, but it does happen. There are many clubs attached to hotels that are subsidised by the hotel and it is counter-productive to have their membership at capacity level. However, if the staff are not encouraged to sell then a feeling of complacency can occur. The presentation of your club by your staff is vital for the sake of morale, appearance and pride. One should always sell for any or all of these reasons.

Membership Turnover

The Numbers Game?

There are those who claim that yearly membership at £25 is desirable. Additional income would be derived from sunbed hire, locker hire, and a vast turnover in memberships, or other ancillary sales available.

The obvious problem, of course, is monitoring the safety of a large number of clients and the wear and tear of your facilities. Usually there is little supervision and staff are encouraged to keep the flow of membership going, with little or no attempt to retain members. This technique is akin to the cut price shops and the 'Two for the Price of One' syndrome. One has to work on the principle that people are constantly looking for a bargain, a cheap sale. If the punters lose interest in the first few weeks, they themselves feel that they haven't really lost out – after all it only cost . . .

Being realistic, however, a £50 annual membership will not sustain any reasonable overheads and we must ask ourselves if we are honestly providing a good or even reasonable service. From experience, people who have laid out even £50 and who wish to train or use those facilities on a regular basis, could feel cheated in today's market where customer service is vital.

From the operator's viewpoint he is working on a very small profit percentage. I only know of a few gym operators who have the skill and experience to make this system work, but with good monitoring of the finances invested frugally and tight control on overheads, the numbers game can work. The American market has proved it. The failure ratio, however, is very high.

This method works on the principle of marketing the gym as a reason for selling your other products. So it is important that there is an abundance of sunbeds, lockers to rent and goods to sell. There would also have to be additional charges for aerobics, sauna, whirlpool and squash. The psychology of this system is that there are more people on the fringe who are not serious about exercising on a regular basis. Membership becomes cyclical and the new influx of interest is always changing. Advertising, therefore, is projected constantly on special offers.

The logical conclusion of this approach, often seen in America, is the same offer being turned around every three months. 'Two for One' on the first quarter, 'Half Membership' on the second quarter and a year's membership with the second year free. The whole procedure would then be re-cycled for the third quarter, with the obvious idea of catching the new wave of interest that is constantly evolving.

Planning Your Open Day

All successful businesses rely on good strategy. It is better to have a bad plan than to have no plan at all. Thinking out your strategy and talking through your plan with your staff or an interested party can save time and expense and reduce the risk of failure.

The open day could prove to be your most consistent, single promotion that you ever do. The main problem is simply getting people through the front door. People do have a fear of entering health clubs. The reason is the popular misconception that all studios are full of Adonis-looking men and fit, slim young women.

The open day means just that, you open the studio to all but in fact close it for use. Your prospective customers then can look without trying, taste without eating and have no fear of having to subject themselves in front of other people. In other words the open day breaks the ice and is a more gentle way of introducing new blood to your studio.

Planning your open day however needs a lot of thought and a great deal of hard work. It is not just a matter of placing an advertisement in the paper, closing the studio down to members and opening up to the public. Let's look at how you should plan your open day.

Selecting the right day is important. We have always felt that Sunday is the day that most people spend at home with the family, so projecting your image to the family as a whole should be carefully planned. It is often advantageous to plan your open day to coincide with the installation of a new piece of equipment or new development.

The Leaflet Drop

This is a marketing exercise that can work very successfully. You simply deliver your advertising leaflets to specific areas.

Making the leaflet drop work for you depends on a number of things and in particular what you are advertising. An offer, providing the offer is a good one, is a winner. Combining the drop with newspaper advertising has a greater chance of success than a drop on its own.

Our own most successful drops have accompanied our open-day promotions, when we have combined a three-point exercise including newspaper advertisments, personal invitations to selected people and a blanket drop in selected areas.

This is the secret of a successful leaflet drop:

- Selection of area – identifying your market
- The most inviting offer – finding something good to sell
- Timing your drop

The months from January to June are good times to drop and in particular late April and May. The old instincts never leave us and the desire to look good for the holiday season is still the greatest motivator for people to begin training. The percentage of success of most promotions is very high at this time of the year, but *our* most successful promotions have always been in August. This is for a specific reason and that is because of our constant efforts to promote our business, year after year, in August. Our open day during this month is easily our most outstanding single promotional success.

The Mail Drop

Another aspect that should be considered is a mail drop. This is the personal invitation and should explain your services and perhaps three highlights of your studio facilities. Direct mail if at all possible should be addressed to the person and not the house, the envelope should be attractive and carry a message. Make your own members aware of the open day and offer them invitations to come down even though you are closed for business. It is a good idea to offer a glass of wine to all visitors and make a point of mentioning this fact in your advertising.

Creating the Right Impression

On the day be generous with flowers, particularly near reception, in the gym and lounge areas. Make sure that you spring-clean the whole complex the night before or better still on the morning of your open day.

All your staff must be versed in the events of the day and if you are going to put on an offer bring them together at least half an hour before you open to iron out any questions that arise. Have some of your staff in track suits to demonstrate the equipment, but predominantly staff should look smart and if possible wear your corporate dress. They should all be prepared to give tours of the gym and be fully conversant with their own area of responsibility.

Your open day is designed to recruit members. Brochures, hand-outs or any information should be available and your reception staff ready to fill out contracts with efficiency.

Always have someone near the entrance to greet people as they come through the door. You could perhaps set up a small table and provide a free raffle for a pair of training shoes or a course of sunbed treatments. By having a raffle you collect names and addresses, a useful way of building up your mailing list.

The staff on reception should specifically have the job of signing up the people who have decided to join.

Preparations for your open day should start weeks in advance and the final week before the open day should be spent putting the finishing touches to the studio.

Promotions

Sunbeds

One of the most profitable services is the sunbed facility. It is an ongoing service but from time to time it needs an injection to create interest and to boost the bookings.

We have a standard charge for a single sunbed treatment (fast tan) of £3. A booking of six works out at £2.50 each (£15), ten sessions for £20. We hold in reserve, for quiet periods, an offer of twenty sessions for £30.

The busy period is from January to June but the demand for sunbeds increases when the sun shines. Who, after all, wants to look milk-bottle white on the beach?

As an alternative and particularly at the opening of your gym or on your open day, try a beach party. Invite people to come along free. Swimwear is the order of the day and each member or prospect can use the sunbeds. The beauty is that wearing swimwear you actually see the effects of the treatment and see that it really does work.

Enrolment Fee and Roll-On Payment

Selling memberships can be made easier by providing a facility that allows clients to pay by monthly instalments. This is a good method, not only to sell memberships but also to keep members.

First arrive at an enrolment fee – say £100. You can explain to the prospect that it is a once only, lifetime payment.

Explain also that the lifetime is as long as they remain members with you and that they will never have to pay again. But if they let their membership lapse then on rejoining they will need to pay the enrolment fee again.

On joining they go onto a monthly payment of say £15. This is done by Bankers Order and the advantages are that your work is decreased and you can explain to the prospect that he or she will have no conflicting bills to pay when renewal comes up (mortgage, household bills, vacations etc).

When selling memberships if a prospect cannot decide, try using the 'first visit offer'. Tell them that if they join today you can cut the enrolment fee by half. If they come back next week or tomorrow, the enrolment fee will have to be paid in full.

Guest Pass Card or Complimentary Membership Card

Once we have accepted the fact that one of the hardest parts of our job is to bring people in through the front door, how do we then go about doing just that?

In addition to our marketing strategies and advertising offers, open days and the rest, we have the guest pass card or complimentary membership card. This facility should be used in the first instance for your own members to bring in a friend who may wish to join. But the card can also be used in a number of different ways. Although you will use the card with some liberalism, treat its distribution as a coveted means of introducing people to your facility.

Make your greatest asset, your existing membership list, work for you. Try and cultivate your members' loyalty and the desire for them to share something they enjoy doing with friends and acquaintances. The complimentary membership card is an ideal way of attracting new members.

In addition to having guest passes on request, we provide our members with a booklet of six guest passes which they can use at their discretion throughout their membership. Of course it is necessary to keep some control and each time a visitor uses a card he or she must sign the visitors' book.

The guest pass card can also be used within your promotional exercises, donating it as a prize for local fetes, beauty competitions, race meetings, sponsored charity events etc. These are excellent ways of keeping your name to the fore and at the same time increasing your potential for bringing in new members.

The complimentary membership card is an excellent means of improving your catchment from telephone sales and improving the business by personal means.

Additional Income

Sometimes called lateral selling, this is the system of making sales from clothing, health foods, T-shirts, gym bags, towels etc.

Anything with your logo on it that is identifiable with your club will have selling potential. The profit margins are relatively low simply due to competition from large manufacturers and chain stores. Sometimes it may not seem worthwhile but those small percentages do add up.

You may think that whilst you are busy selling a T-shirt you could be selling memberships. Remember that everything that goes out with your name on it is free advertising. In addition, having your name on these products raises your credibility.

Marketing additional products can have disadvantages. Beware of buying large stocks and having too much capital tied up. Remember that leisure wear is now part of the fashion industry with a constantly changing product. Your customers will only buy once and you will not have the passing trade of the High Street shops. It is still, however, an essential part of your business.

Maintaining Membership

People

Our business is about people and the single most important ingredient of business is personal relations. We are indeed in a selling business and essentially we are selling ourselves. Our clients are our business. Creating the right atmosphere goes a long way towards membership retention. The struggle in today's market place is becoming more and more aggressive and more competitive. A membership lost is a membership wasted; every effort must be made to create a congenial atmosphere with an attitude of friendliness and attentiveness showing that you care for your clients. This helps to build loyalty. However, it is not sufficient on its own, other incentives are sometimes necessary – small gifts for continuous membership, free sunbed treatments on renewal, corporate key-rings – to create a sense of identity. Your customers need to feel a part of the club and anything that facilitates this is going to promote your business.

Some years ago we realised that the only time we made contact with our members was when they came to us to train or when we sent out membership renewals. The first thing we did was to organise a free gift on renewal, we also implemented Christmas cards and then formulated a system of collecting dates of birth so that we could send out birthday cards. We now use a newsletter and the occasional social evening. At the start of our 'wooing the customer' campaign we changed our invoice system by adding colour, making it softer, and added a sentence thanking them for their continued custom, all designed to cement good relations.

Product

Keeping your customers interested is a continuous process; there must never be a time when you relax this vigil. Your facilities are your showcase and just as the shopkeeper or superstore changes its showcase or shop window so should you. If you were to walk into Marks & Spencer today and then again in a few weeks there would be inevitable changes in display, fashion layouts and colours. In our case it need not always be expensive and the changes can be subtle or vast but do it you must. One of our greatest enemies is boredom, keep interest alive by continual change.

New products are always coming on to the market and can put a tremendous amount of pressure on your finance. A lot of thought must be given to what you buy and what you are prepared to sell. Some of your equipment will last for many years, some will quickly become unfashionable. Your judgement is paramount but it is not just your equipment that will attract customers.

Presentation is important: attitudes; decor; variety; cleanliness; maintenance; staff; service and standards should all hold equal standing when product is being considered. The best studio will always attract the most customers.

Profits

The bottom line is, of course, making money. Making money is not that hard to do, spending it comes a lot easier and

the balance of payments, profit and loss or income and outgoings are the difficult side of business. Your problems will arise with the allocation of your takings. All things being equal and following the rules you will make profits. How you spend your profits is entirely up to your judgement, but make sure you reinvest sufficient to retain your hard-won members.

You Have Just Been Sold An 85p Spoon

A good friend of mine and an excellent salesman claims that he never sells anyone anything, but he helps a lot of people to buy. The art of selling is, of course, to have your prospect buy without feeling that he has been sold to.

The other night my wife and I went to a local pizza restaurant. One of the excellent dishes they serve is an Avocado and Prawn Gratinée covered in a beautiful prawn sauce. They serve it with a knife and fork. It really is a delicious dish but have you ever tried eating sauce with a knife and fork?

Not wanting to miss out on the prawn sauce I asked Harry for a spoon. 'Certainly, Ken' he said 'I will get you the spoon. But why don't you mop it up with some bread?' – an open-ended question. What a good idea, I thought. His next question was not open-ended but a closed or tie-down question. 'Would you like pitta bread or would you like garlic bread?' 'I will have some pitta bread please, Harry.' Two minutes later I was presented with a portion of piping hot pitta bread and also the spoon. It dawned on me at that precise moment that I had just bought an 85p spoon. The price Harry charges for his pitta and garlic bread is 85p per portion. Like my other friend – the excellent salesman – Harry too had helped me to buy.

3 Day-to-Day Working

The Right Image

Your attitude as a health club owner is very important. You will be seen as the archangel by many. It is also a little unfortunate that some people look upon us with some suspicion and think that we are not quite respectable. There was some degree of bad publicity a few years ago due to the 'slap and tickle' syndrome which attached us to the sauna and massage parlours in some towns and cities. Regardless of how well you run your business some outsiders will unfortunately take this attitude.

You will be expected to be moral without being moralistic, fit without being fanatical. You will need to soak up people's problems, giving advice of a medical as well as a physiological nature. Smoking, drinking and the rest of man's sins are just for mere mortals, not for the gym owner. So take care and remember that whilst in the goldfish bowl your actions are seen from every angle.

Your role demands that you are always seen as your clients want to see you. So it is important that you embody your type of establishment, be it just a gym or the more up-market health club. But you must never forget your commitment to your customers and your obligations to your staff and yourself.

Remember also that your social life is not your own. The health club boss should never be seen propping up the bar or eating junk food. Your language and behaviour will come under scrutiny in public. Once people become acquainted with you, you will be constantly asked for ways of reducing their waistlines or some remedy for their aching back.

This attention, at first, can be very flattering but after a few years of saying the same thing over and over again it will try your patience. The rewards however easily outweigh the disadvantages. Seeing the transformation in people's health attitudes to life and the building of better bodies holds no measure. If you are good at your job, the successful, the famous and the media will seek you out. Over the years we have assisted some of the best. Peter Reid, when playing for Bolton Wanderers sought our help when injured. The legendary squash player, Jonah Barrington, was a frequent visitor to our studio as was rugby league and superstar Des Drummond. And our Hall of Fame displays dozens of famous personalities, some of them champions locally and many who are of international acclaim.

Perhaps more important, if you are good, is that the experts themselves, doctors, surgeons, coaches and satisfied customers, will all recommend and refer people to you, the expert in your field.

Yes, the job can be quite rewarding. You may even make some money!

Management

John Betteridge, one of our chief lecturers on our NABBA training courses talks of hard rules and soft advice. One has to be hard on rules. They are important and there is always, always a way of implementing those hard rules. Be firm but strong. Think in terms of sandwiching your criticism between chunks of praise. Soft can really be hard or, paradoxically, hard can be soft. Managing staff is not much different from managing your club. Apply the same principles to how you handle your own personnel and how you handle your clients.

Even in small businesses we can lose touch. Make sure that not only do you talk to your staff but more important, you listen. Spend some time with each member of your staff and you will reap the dividends. Practise what you preach. It is important that your staff have respect for you. Listening and acting accordingly will raise that respect. Mike Chaet of Marketing Management Services in Montana has a simple way of putting it. 'Walk Your Talk'. And that is exactly what you should be doing. The walkabout will be the most important exercise you will do each day in terms of productivity. Each part of the studio and every aspect must be inspected every day. By observing on a daily basis and acting on what you see, standards will be maintained. The cleanliness and constant maintenance of your establishment can never be over-emphasised. Listen to what your members are saying and develop a rapport. Learn to call them by their first names. Respect their requests and constantly keep in touch. Make sure too that you write down everything that needs to be done from small repairs to the cleanliness of your equipment and facilities. By being seen to be productive you will gain respect. Management is leadership.

Talking to your staff and talking to your clients is extremely important. More important however is listening and seeing. Look, listen and then talk. You have two ears, two eyes and one mouth. Use them in that proportion. Always be honest with yourself, your staff and your clients. Work within the realms of reality. However, if it can be done – do it.

Requests from staff for higher wages and demands for better facilities from your clients will constantly put you under pressure. Consider all, and if it is realistic then do it. Listen to the complaints and acknowledge them. If it is a genuine complaint and its rectification would improve your club – then do it. Constant improvements to your club will improve morale for both client and staff. When that happens you will be on the receiving end of the praise. Listen to that too and respond with a thank you.

All this takes time. Organising your time produces greater efficiency and productivity and brings respect from the people around you. But time management requires discipline and the discipline starts with you writing down all the chores that are to be carried out each day. The simplest way is to formulate your list each night for the following day. Number the jobs in order of priority and carry out the jobs each day one by one. In the event that all your jobs are not completed then add them on to your next day's chores, again in order of importance. It is inevitable that you are going to push the less important jobs to the end of your list. If the jobs are not very important then don't put them on your list in the first place.

Staff

Building a team around you is a constant endeavour. How you select your staff can make the difference between a smooth-running organisation and one that is constantly fraught with problems. Choosing the right people for the right job can only be successful if you plan carefully. Try and maintain a good cross-section of age groups to mirror the ages of your clientele. It is inconceivable to have young, trendy staff throughout your organisation. You will never be able to be at the gym all the time so it is obvious that you will need someone to fill your role when you are not there. Do not make yourself indispensable.

At present instructors do not need professional qualifications. However, since the inception of NABBA Instructors' Courses in 1985, employers are increasingly looking for this qualification when employing staff.

To give you an idea of the numbers of staff necessary allow approximately one member of staff to every 100 members. In a gym with 1,300–2,000 members you would need two male and two female full-time instructors as well as part-time instructors to cover busy periods. It would be useful to have a couple of people on standby in case of illness or for particularly busy periods. Additional staff

would be necessary for reception and office work.

A physiotherapist would only be employed by a very large club. It is wise to find out who the best physiotherapist is in your area, as you should always refer anything other than minor injuries to them.

Staff training requires skill and patience. The role of each individual must be made clear from the outset. The largest and the smallest organisations are totally reliant on good staff. More important, however, is your ability to organise them. Planning is essential and with a small operation tends to happen as you go along. The more conscientious your staff are the less problems you will have, but from a communication point of view, regular staff meetings are a must.

The front desk and reception area give an all-important first impression

These are the times when problems, large or small, can be talked out and clear indictions given of what has to be done and in what order of importance.

The Front Desk

The person who works your reception area must keep that area clean and tidy and must present the right image at all times. It is the first impression that counts and for your clients to be greeted with a smile and a hello followed by their name will do wonders for your renewal rate and morale.

The front desk should always be kept free from anything that is not conducive to its function. To see someone lounging, disinterested, sloppy in appearance, maybe drinking coffee, ignoring customers and just talking to friends will quickly spread the wrong atmosphere throughout your club or gym.

If you are not able to work reception yourself, take care when selecting the person you wish to represent you. The responsibility of handling money and the simple but important daily sheet, telephone calls and booking appointments will fall on him. This is the heart of your business, everything revolves around and starts at the front desk.

Records

A certain amount of paperwork is necessary to keep your gym running smoothly and to keep your accounts in order. The following forms are a few of the ways to keep your paperwork as simple and efficient as possible. It is possible to computerise your records and packages can be tailored to your individual needs.

Receipt Pad
You must keep a record of everything

Fig 8 Receipt

that is taken in payment and a simple carbonated pad serves the purpose admirably. The customer is given the top copy and you keep the other copy.

Daily Cash Analysis
Everything that is received in payment is then entered onto the Daily Cash Analysis Sheet. In this way you have a record of everything which has been paid in, entered under different headings.

Takings Book
The totals from the Daily Cash Analysis are transferred to the Takings Book which is divided into the same headings. These figures will be needed by your accountants.

Ledger of Members
Details of members and their membership payments are kept in the

BOLTON HEALTH STUDIO

SHEET No. 325

DATE ....18ᵗʰ May........ 19 88...

DAILY CASH RECEIVED AND ANALYSIS

←———— BASIC INFORMATION ————→ | ←———————— ANALYSIS ————————→

Subs No.	MEMBER'S NAME	TOTAL RECEIVED	Full Annual Subscription	3 Months Subscription	Instalment of Subscription	Sports Goods	Locker Hire	Books	SUNBEDS	BEAUTY	COSMETICS	RESTAURANT TAKINGS	FITNESS TEST.
5552	R.S. Howe E/Fee	25.00			25.00								
4568	S. Denton	41.02			41.02								
	Beauty	8.75								8.75			
	Buchner FTS	3.00							3.00				
	S.B	1.00							1.00				
	Beauty	5.75								5.75			
	"	8.60								8.60			
	"	3.00								3.00			
	"	5.40								5.40			
	"	6.25								6.25			
	Joanne FTS	3.00							3.00				
	Beauty	4.90								4.90			
	"	10.15								10.15			
	"	9.80								9.80			
	Beattie 10 FTS	25.00							20.00				
	Beauty	10.20								10.20			
	"	9.25								9.25			
	"	5.75								5.75			
5155	P. Zetley E/Fee	25.00			25.00								

Fig 9 Daily cash analysis

Ledger of Members. A separate page should be kept for each membership sold and details of the member's name, address and payments are kept.

Member's Record Card
A card – about 15×10cm (6×4in) – should be kept for each member with name, address, membership number and payment details. This card makes it easier to send out renewal notices when they become due.

Contract
An agreement is entered into by the gym and each new member. This is done on a special agreement form which needs to be drawn up for you by a solicitor.

Membership Card
Each new member should be issued with a membership card showing his/her membership number which should be shown also on the Member's Record Card and Ledger of Members.

Fig 10 Member's record card

Invoice
You should have an invoice drawn up for membership renewals. A tear-off slip is useful. The member completes the details required and returns it to the gym with his renewal payment.

Signing-In Sheet
It is important that you keep a signing-in sheet at reception so that you have a record of all the people who have come into the gym on a particular day. You will find this useful for checking who is in at any time and also for monitoring numbers attending.

Standards

Over the years we have seen many health clubs launched in a blaze of publicity, sporting tremendous facilities, sparkling equipment, modern, tasteful decor and offering very attractive terms. The owners were genuinely ambitious and full of dreams and aspirations to provide the very best amenities and service.

NAME: MR. JAMES R.BROWN.   MEMB. No. 12345

	1st Yr. B.O.MONTHLY.	2nd Yr.	3rd Yr.	4th Yr.	5th Yr.
ADDRESS 12.Smith Street, Bolton. BL2 5EB	25.5.89R*				

30 Mawdsley Street, Bolton, Lancashire. BL1 1LF. Telephone: Bolton 22540 and 389290

INVOICE   VAT No. 337 4038 62   17th May, 19 88

To Annual Membership Fee due.............. 25th May,1988 ....

Yearly......... £ 124.35   Quarterly.... £

+ VAT @   £ 18.65   + VAT @   £

Total........... £ 143.00   Total............ £   N/A

Your renewal is now due and to keep your membership in tact and avoid the coming increases in subscription rates the above amount must be paid by.................25th May, 1988.................................

I understand my Annual Subscription falls due on........... 25th May,1988

I wish to keep my membership intact for a further twelve month period and pay

        ☐ annually   ☐ quarterly

I enclose......................which allows me FULL MEMBERSHIP of Bolton Health Studio.

B.H.S. Membership No. .... 12344 - J.Jones. ....

Signed...

PLEASE RETURN THIS PORTION WITH YOUR SUBSCRIPTION.

Fig 11 Invoice

Almost all of those health clubs have either closed or at the very least standards have fallen. There are a number of very good reasons for this and hopefully the guidance from this book will at least highlight the major pitfalls of the gym business.

Falling standards are responsible for 90 per cent of the failures in the gym business. Standards fall because of lack of funds, loss of interest, lack of staff training, inadequate supervision and a failure to recognise the day-to-day gradual erosion of those standards. Each and every member of your staff must be alerted to the importance of every aspect of the presentation of your gym.

Hygiene

There is a consistent theme nine times out of every ten when someone reports that a gym has folded. Part of the conversation always reveals that the club had become dirty and scruffy.

Cleanliness is of paramount importance. Keeping your gym clean, tidy and well maintained is a constant daily effort. Wherever you expect people to gather in numbers or groups, you must expect dirt. The more people you have under one roof, the worse the problem becomes. Just imagine what it is like with 200 people under one roof.

Hospitals have enormous problems maintaining sterile conditions. Put one person to one room and the risk is minimal. Put twenty beds in one room and make it into a ward and then you have problems. It is the same in restaurants. Keeping germs to a minimum with only two people eating – no problem. Get fifty people together and hygiene has top priority.

People exude germs. This is never more evident than in your shower area. Water from a shower rinses approximately 300 million bacteria from the body in the first five minutes. Many of these bacteria can be harmful. Athlete's foot is a common fungus found in shower areas. Keep risks to a minimum by spraying at least twice a day with an anti-fungal disinfectant. Remember it is relatively easy to prevent, but extremely hard to eradicate.

Appearances play an important part in your image. On one occasion the gullies in our shower area had acquired an ingrained discolouration. We had tried all methods of erasing the problem, even sand blasting and application of acid without effect. We finally gave up until someone mentioned the fact that it *looked* like scum, which it wasn't. It left us no alternative but to retile the area. We came to the conclusion that from the customer's point of view there is very little difference between something looking dirty and actually being dirty.

Security

An ever-increasing problem is security. The more people there are in one area the greater the problem. People are remarkably careless when comfortable. The better your facility, the safer your members will feel , and the more secure they feel the more vulnerable they are.

We go to great lengths to provide a locker service that costs our members nothing. A simple deposit on a locker key returnable at the end of the visit and all items are safe. People will still however insist on leaving even valuable things around to be pounced on by the habitual thief. When we get a spate of thefts it is invariably a run of the same type of clothing or item.

Some years ago we had someone with a colourful shirt fetish. The shirts had to be colourful to be stolen. We even detected who the thief was. We set the usual traps but he had the instinct of a fox and evaded all our efforts. Because of all our efforts and pressure he eventually left the club, and the pilfering of colourful shirts (size was no object) stopped.

There are a few guidelines that may help you to minimise the problem. Always try and issue lockers or have a security service at reception, perhaps both. Write into your information for members that theft can be a problem and discreetly point out to new members that there is always the possibility that this can occur. Ask your members to co-operate by being alert to the situation.

Thefts tend to go in spates and after a couple of incidents start to form a pattern. Check your signing-in sheet to see who is in at that particular time. In almost every case when thefts start it is due to a new recruit. Thieves are compulsive, so if nothing has been happening it stands to reason that the established members are in the clear. By a process of elimination you can very quickly narrow the suspects down to a few people. It is at this stage that you can start leaving traps around. Play it very low key in the early stages and never make your move until you are absolutely sure. Always inform the police, even at the early stages.

A large percentage of the goods that go missing are in fact misplaced. I once informed the police that £60 had gone missing from the right-hand back pocket of a client's trousers. The whole changing room had been searched and even other people's bags etc. It was very embarrassing for the client when the money was found in the left-hand back pocket of his trousers!

A Typical Day

No matter how well you plan you will find that there are certain peak hours during the course of the day. The peak evening period puts tremendous pressure on the shower areas; nearly 65 per cent of clients will attend at this time. The peak times are:

UK   7am–9am and 6pm–8pm
USA   6am–8am and 4pm–6pm

A typical gym in England would open at 7am, Monday to Saturday, with 'Early Bird' mixed training until 10am. At 10am one gym would continue with mixed training and training in the other gym would be segregated. The flow of clients would be continuous until about 2pm when until 4.30pm the gym would be very quiet. The numbers would begin to build up to a peak from 6.30pm to 8pm. The gym would finally close at 10pm.

There would be various group classes and aerobics and 20 Minute Total Body Workout programmes going on throughout the peak evening period.

Recent indications are that early morning training is becoming increasingly popular following the American model.

4 Exercise Programmes

Group Classes

You must be prepared to provide the classes the customer wants. As the health business expands we have found that we must improvise and provide not only gym facilities but classes, advice and the latest in fitness assessment. Above all, safety is of paramount importance now that group classes have become an essential part of most good gyms. A good instructor should be able to take the following elements in his or her stride.

Personality

On taking charge, the instructor technically becomes an expert. His/her knowledge will be constantly sought and for this reason he/she must acquire a knowledge of basic anatomy, physiology, diet, first aid and general safety rules.

Qualifications

The instructor must have a sense of dignity and leadership. It is obviously necessary to be fit, but because the instructor is involved in the taking of classes and is not wholly involved in actually performing the exercises, his/her level of fitness can, and sometimes does fall. It is essential to be aware of this and maintain an acceptable level of fitness. The instructor is responsible for the members of the class at all times and should be aware of that responsibility.

Enthusiasm

This is extremely important and very, very hard to maintain at a high level constantly. It is of vital importance that each class should be approached as if it were the first (not the umpteenth one that day). If the instructor fails to be enthusiastic and fails to communicate this enthusiasm, then the class will soon lose interest. The instructor must be seen to be enjoying and deriving actual benefit from the class.

Taking a Class

The prospective instructor should learn projection, give the necessary instruction, warn and single out individuals who might need additional help, observe the age and fitness level of each member of the class and have the ability to address a class. He/she should get to know the class and acquire the ability to select the person to 'put up front' in order that class members might identify with that person as regards timing and form. He/she should be taught to impress upon the class that the members should follow 'the leader'. This makes the instructor's job easier in that he/she can identify the levels or degrees of fitness of each individual, eg if some members do not keep in time, go the wrong way, perform the exercise wrongly, or if the degree of movement is less than other members of the class.

Control and Discipline

The instructor needs to control each individual in the class, ie although it is a class of say twenty people, they are, in fact, twenty individuals. In order for the class to acquire the maximum benefit the instructor needs to control, keep order and, to a certain degree, discipline the members of the class. It is extremely

Aerobics

Fatigues — the male equivalent of aerobics —
proved that men were willing to take part in
large numbers

important that the instructor circulates throughout the class. He/she must have contact with each and every member within that class and must always be seen to be in control.

Equipment

Always ensure that the equipment and tapes are checked before commencing the class. Always dress neatly, tidily and be clean and smart.

Concern for Class Members

It is essential, on every occasion, that a warning is given to beginners. It is the instructor's job to note the level of fitness of each class member. It is imperative that the class is asked who the beginners are and that the class members are warned to work within their own capabilities and to their own level of fitness. This warning will be repeated many, many times, but it is absolutely necessary to go through this procedure at the beginning of every single class. The instructor must be seen to give the warning in a safe and measured way and to care for each individual's welfare.

Aerobics

Aerobics have attracted much criticism over the last few years due to the number of injuries sustained. However, many of the injuries were sustained by people who were unfit or were only casual attenders. Ironically many instructors suffered due to the overuse of certain movements.

The aerobic boom meant that many instructors were not properly prepared and had little experience in prescribing exercise. Ballistic-type movements were the cause of most injuries to both the unfit and instructors. Therefore jumping and bouncing should be kept to a minimum. Slow controlled movements, with straight legs are preferable.

Many dancers and dance teachers wrongly confused exercise prescription with dance prescription and automatically assumed that what was good for dancers was good for the general public. Physiologically what is right for a dancer can be totally wrong for an unsupple middle-aged person. And the general belief that a dance instructor has more qualifications in this field than say a nurse, football coach or army PT instructor is wrong. All are, of course, experts but only in their particular field. There are many people who have graduated from these and other professions to be competent and safe teachers of exercise. The whirlwind of 'Fondaism' and dance-type movement bore little resemblance to the real world. Only commonsense and careful thinking will lead to a balance that will be acceptable to people of all ages and both sexes for music-orientated exercise classes.

Setting up an aerobic class can be a very time-consuming exercise. For every minute on your tape, it takes a minimum of an hour's work. A half-hour tape will take you thirty hours to put together.

First and foremost your class should have balance: warm-up, general all-round bodywork, aerobic section and cool-down. Look for the three S's – suppleness, strength and stamina – with a balance of exercise to cover all the areas.

Warm-up

The warm-up could start with variations on head rolls – side to side, forward and back. Gradually work down the body working the shoulders – shrugging, rotating, together and alternately. Torso movements follow next – twisting gently, lateral movements (side bends) and even rotating movements. Stretch gently to warm the lower back and hamstrings by bending forward – emphasising the slow stretch in this vulnerable area. Finally the legs, with squat and lunge movements, incorporating calf raises to complete your warm-up.

Content

The same principle can be followed for the content of the class, gradually working down the body.

Start with the shoulders (eg arm circles) and then go on to torso movements with twisting and side movements. Then upper and lower abdominals, waist and lower back. It is essential to work the four abdominal areas – upper and lower abdominals, obliques and lower back.

Move onto the legs, hips and thighs, followed by the aerobic section.

The aerobic section should be mid- or three-quarters of the way through your programme and should allow for perhaps one section of twisting or stretching before going into the cool-down. To derive any benefit from the aerobic section it needs to be a minimum of 10–12 minutes and naturally a little more for the advanced.

Cool-down

If your cool-down is immediately after the aerobic section then it needs to be a prolonged one – 6 or 7 minutes. It will only need to be 3 to 4 minutes if your stretching or waist work follows the aerobic section.

Age

Take the age factor into consideration. Too much high-impact work will quickly bring about injuries. More slow stretching is needed along with more low-impact exercises and no jumping.

Beginners

The same principle applies with beginners. Always monitor each individual and do not let them do too much.

Music

Do not fall into the trap of just picking music that *you* like. Music should be a motivating factor but it should also fit the exercises at a pace that is acceptable for correct movements.

When grouping your exercises think in terms of easy/hard, alternating a strenuous exercise with a relatively easy exercise. The average person is not an athlete. Putting people through it will only last so long before they begin to drift away. People think they like to be pushed but the thought of pain will push people away from you.

Try and look at as many people's classes as you can. Copy the good parts but also remember to impose your personality onto your classes. Above all, try not to be *too* clever by expecting people to have rhythm when they don't have it, stamina when they are not fit, and co-ordination when they are without it.

Fitness Assessment

Fitness Assessment is in its infancy and you must not confuse it with health checks. Fitness assessment plays a very positive role in the gyms of today. The tests include measuring VO_2 capacity and the ability to utilise available oxygen, fat-fold test, blood pressure, strength and weight. The following equipment is required:

Computer and software
Bicycle ergometer
Blood pressure unit
Skinfold calipers
Heart-rate monitor
Sit and reach box or flexibility measuring device

left and below Fitness assessment

Scales (weight)
Height measure (optional)
Lung function – peak flow meter (optional)
Grip strength – dynomometer (optional)
Leg and back strength dynomometer (optional)
Stopwatch or timer thermometer
(Suppliers – Cardio Kinetics, Cranlea, The Sandpits, Acadia Road, Bournville, Birmingham B30 2AH Tel 021 472 0361.)

The assessment is a guide to the instructor on how to tailor the level of exercise to each individual. There is, however, a certain measure of feedback on the state of health of the subject so if the person is excessively overweight or his blood pressure is high or the VO_2 reading is very low, then extreme caution is necessary and referral to a doctor

would be in order.

The assessment can also provide useful information for working out exercise programmes. More stamina work if the VO_2 is low, or more stretching needed and so on. Naturally we cannot give an opinion on blood pressure readings but in the event that all is not well then we can again refer to a doctor. The greatest asset of the assessment is the motivation factor. Regular assessments every three months, provide targets for the pupil to follow. There should always be a consultation at each assessment and directional training advice given on diet, motivation and therapy. A charge can be made for each assessment and there is good reason for giving the first one free. People will come back for two, three or perhaps regular assessments if encouraged to do so.

The price you charge is dependent upon a number of factors. Firstly, the depth of consultation and how much time it takes. If an instructor administers the test you would expect to charge less than if you had qualified medical staff. An exercise physiologist with good qualifications would charge less than a doctor but more than an instructor. Secondly, if it is a computer read-out you would demand more than if your calculations were read from charts. Thirdly, a private room is a must, but if you are forced to tuck the area into a corner with a curtain around, this would diminish the service and, of course, your chargeable fee.

It will be necessary in the near future to make this service a standard procedure and include the price in every membership fee.

20 Minute Total Body Workout

We first introduced the 20 Minute Total Body Workout early in 1987 (see Fig. 12).

The reasons were numerous. Firstly, seeing our membership increase, secondly, with the installation of Fitness 1 (our new gym) and the increased volume of equipment, it was necessary to control the flow of people. Thirdly, the 20 Minute Total Body Workout fitted in with our award assessment programme. The most important thing about this workout was that people identified themselves with a start and finish programme by emphasising the time as opposed to the number of exercises.

In the past we made out programmes for individuals and gave them a number of sets and repetitions. Sometimes we would prescribe the set system, perhaps circuit-type training, PHA or sequence training and variations on all of those themes. On all of these systems you can of course set targets and implement a time structure to promote interest and individual motivation. Universal's Super Circuit is an excellent example of this system.

We attempted, with the 20 Minute Total Body Workout, to identify the importance of the time element and the psychology behind it. We all find it hard to get going. Even the most dedicated athletes find it hard to get started. Once under way the workout becomes infinitely easier. Having only twenty minutes ahead of you reduces many barriers and helps to keep you going once started. By prescribing alternative exercises for different body parts, the 20 Minute Total Body Workout can be varied to suit each individual.

The strength of this system is its time factor. Anyone can find twenty minutes, even the busiest of business men and housewives or the most time conscious. It is also an excellent means of selling memberships.

Formulating a Programme

This is something you will be asked to do frequently. Actually writing out or putting together a programme is a simple, easy matter. But it is quite extraordinary how people interpret their own basic needs and put them into someone else's schedule.

There is a logical pattern of application once you have determined the needs of the client. You must first screen your client and arrive at a figure/physique analysis. Determine at this stage what the client wants. If you have not already asked the relevant questions then this is the time to do so. Remember that you are writing out a schedule to suit them. Weigh up what they need, not what *you* want.

At this level we are dealing with a basic

Fig 12 The 20 Minute Total Body Workout programme

programme. Over the years, if you are still instructing, you will get many, many strange requests. But generally, for now, we will put them into four categories. These are:

1 Increase or body-build
2 Slim or reduce
3 Get fit or tone-up
4 Train for a specific sport

We have to deal with basic weight training, keeping generally to the basic exercises. For example, if someone wants to build up the arms (biceps) then the logical exercise to turn to is the two hands barbell curl. It is totally illogical to prescribe the bent-over close-grip barbell concentration curl. The first exercise will do everything that is expected of it. It is easy to apply, uncomplicated in its execution and easy to demonstrate. That simple rule applies

Try for your award of excellence on one of these
20 minute programmes *for your Bronze, Silver, & Gold Awards*

20 min. total body workout	Alternative	Alternative
Bike, Jogger, Rowing - 6 mins	**Bike, Jogger, Rowing - 6 mins**	**Bike, Jogger, Rowing - 6 mins**
13 Shoulder Press . . . . . 12 Reps.	12 Bench Press . . . . 12 Reps.	12 Bench Press . . . . 12 Reps.
6 Leg Press . . . . 12 Reps.	18 Squats . . . . 12 Reps.	11 Thigh Curl . . . . 12 Reps.
4 Pull Downs . . . . 12 Reps.	4 Reverse Pulls . . . . 12 Reps.	23 Side Shoulder Raise . . . 12 Reps.
22 Upper Abs . . . . 25 Reps.	21 Calf Raise . . . . 20 Reps.	21 Calf Raise . . . . 20 Reps.
7 Curls . . . . 12 Reps.	13 Shoulder Press . . . . . 12 Reps.	4 Pulldowns . . . . 12 Reps.
21 Calf Raises . . . . 20 Reps.	10 Thigh Ext. . . . . 12 Reps.	10 Thigh Ext. . . . . 12 Reps.
12 Bench Press . . . . 12 Reps.	7 Preacher Curls . . . . . . 12 Reps.	15 Curls (Pully) . . . . . . 12 Reps.
11 Leg Curl. . . . . 12 Reps.	11 Thigh Curls . . . . 12 Reps.	18 Squats Mch. . . . . 12 Reps.
16 Tri Push Downs. . . . 12 Reps.	9 Back Mch. . . . . 15 Reps.	8 Tri Pushdowns. . . . . . 12 Reps.
15 Upright Rows. . . . . . 12 Reps.	22 Upper Abs . . . . 25 Reps.	Boards-Sit ups . . . . 25 Reps.
9 Back Mch. . . . . 15 Reps.	8 Tri Pushdowns. . . . . . 12 Reps.	15 Reverse Curls . . . . . . 12 Reps.
10 Thigh Ext. . . . . 12 Reps.	15 Reverse Curls . . . . . . 12 Reps.	Pole-Twist Bar . . . . 1 Min.
Pole Twists . . . . 1 Min.	20 Lower Abs . . . . 25 Reps.	
	Twist Bar . . . . 1 Min.	

Select a poundage that allows approx. 12 repetitions and train to failure.

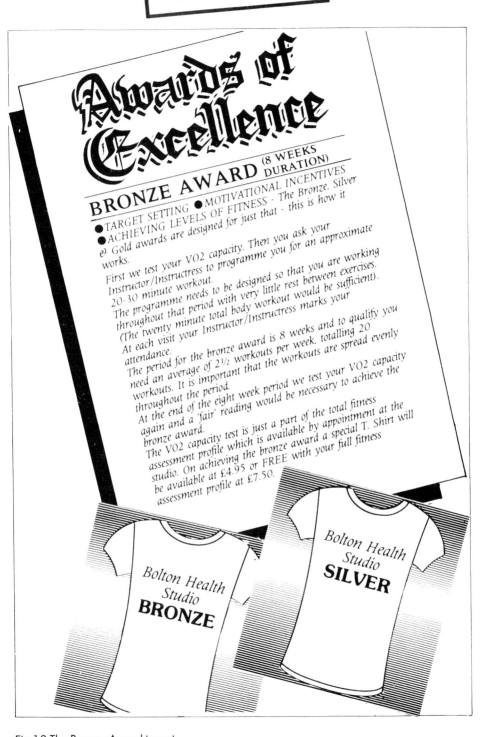

Awards of Excellence

BRONZE AWARD (8 WEEKS DURATION)

- TARGET SETTING ● MOTIVATIONAL INCENTIVES
- ACHIEVING LEVELS OF FITNESS - The Bronze, Silver
- & Gold awards are designed for just that - this is how it works.

First we test your VO2 capacity. Then you ask your Instructor/Instructress to programme you for an approximate 20-30 minute workout.

The programme needs to be designed so that you are working throughout that period with very little rest between exercises. (The twenty minute total body workout would be sufficient).

At each visit your Instructor/Instructress marks your attendance.

The period for the bronze award is 8 weeks and to qualify you need an average of 2½ workouts per week, totalling 20 workouts. It is important that the workouts are spread evenly throughout the period.

At the end of the eight week period we test your VO2 capacity again and a 'fair' reading would be necessary to achieve the bronze award.

The VO2 capacity test is just a part of the total fitness assessment profile which is available by appointment at the studio. On achieving the bronze award a special T. Shirt will be available at £4.95 or FREE with your full fitness assessment profile at £7.50.

Bolton Health Studio **BRONZE**

Bolton Health Studio **SILVER**

Fig 13 The Bronze Award target

to every single exercise when making out a programme for the beginner. It is as simple as that. Select one exercise for each body part, moderate repetitions, moderate weights. Remember your analysis. If you have a woman of thirty-five years who has two children and has not exercised for quite some time, then she is not going to be doing the same as a twenty-year-old girl who has been involved in sport, or indeed a twenty-year-old who has *not* been involved in sport.

Not everyone comes to the gym for the same reasons. There is, however, one single common denominator. No one is completely happy with the shape they are in. Your figure/physique analysis is going to tell you how to make out your programme. Generally speaking you will be dealing with requests to build-up, slim-down or tone-up. The variations on the three categories are, of course, infinite but it is sufficient at this stage to stay with the basics.

Programme for Building-Up

Beginners should start with only one set of each exercise and then progressively increase, depending on age and ability, to three sets, building up to 8–10 repetitions with perhaps 12 repetitions for the squat and 20 repetitions for the stiff arm pull-over, abdominals etc.

Sit-ups	8–20
Leg raises	8–20
Side bends	20–50
Press behind neck	8
Bench press	8
Pull-downs or	
bent over rowing	8
Squats	12
Stiff arm pull-over	20
Tricep push down	10
Barbell curl	10

It is worth noting that there is only one

exercise per body part (excepting abdominals). Each exercise generally works the mass. Squats are placed towards the end of the programme and by this time the body is fully warmed-up. Stiff arm pull-over immediately follows the squats and is utilised totally as a rib stretching, breathing exercise. The arm exercises are left until last because if arm work is put at the beginning of the programme, then chest, back and shoulder work is diminished.

All exercises should be done in good style. The breathing sequence should be:

- **Breathe in before the effort**
- **Breathe out during the effort**

Programme for Slimming or Reducing

A programme for slimming or reducing would naturally involve more repetitions and possibly more abdominal exercises. In the case of a woman whose figure required more work on hips and thighs, the exercises would be pitched in that direction. So an average, moderately healthy woman who wishes to reduce, but with special attention to hips and thighs, would have a programme looking like this:

Warm-up	
Sit-ups	8 increasing to 20
Leg raises	8 increasing to 20
Twists	20 increasing to 50
Thigh machine or	
side kicks	15 or 50
Leg machine or	
free squat	10 or 10–20
Bench press	8
Pull-downs	8
Up rowing	8
Kneeling side	
kicks	20 increasing to 50
Alternate toe	
touching	15 increasing to 25
Side bends	20 increasing to 50
Twister	20 increasing to 50

Depending on the availability of machines, you could substitute exercises to work certain areas, hip machine, squat machine, thigh extension and so on. The emphasis as you can see is on waist, hips and thighs, but also includes upper body work to give overall conditioning. You must also assess the ability of the individual to complete maximum repetitions.

Programme for Toning-up

Conditioning is a repeat of the building-up programme. There is no emphasis here on increasing poundages to maximum stimulation of the muscle group. Increasing circulation is enough – moderate poundages throughout with perhaps slight increase in repetitions.

The two schedules given are examples of how to formulate a programme for someone with a standardised request. Ninety-five per cent of the people coming through the door will be in those categories and are therefore fairly easy to deal with.

Programme for Specific Sports

General Guide:

1 Use framework
2 Supplement the sports training
3 Beware duplication or giving too much training
4 Find out what other training/coaching the client is undertaking
5 Consider speed of movements
6 Consider time in sporting year
7 Consider age/fitness of client

Example:
Warm-up – stretching/mobility work
Abdominals – sit-ups and crunches
Shoulder press or press behind neck
Squat or leg press
Bench press

Bent over rowing or vertical row machine
Dead lift or back machine
Barbell curl or curl machine
Calf raises
Cool-down

This programme could be related to a number of different sports like soccer, cycling or rugby. It is a general strength building programme for sport.

Summary
Consider:

1 Knowledge of athlete
2 'S' factors
3 Training principles
4 Training techniques
5 Training year

Framework
1 Analyse needs of the sport
2 Analyse client need (position he/she plays)
3 Ensure
  ● Warm-up
  ● Flexibility
  ● Strength   phases
  ● Endurance
  ● Cool-down
4 Emphasise **all over** body training, ie major muscles and stomach
5 Emphasise client weaknesses
6 'S' factors
  ● Strength
  ● Suppleness
  ● Speed
  ● Skill

Cardiovascular Exercise

Within a few short weeks the client will in all probability make excellent progress. Muscle tone and body condition will improve and a feeling of well-being will

The jogging boom is something more than running marathons. Electronic running machines have made running part of man's life-style in and out of doors

certainly be experienced. The programmes will be sufficient to help the beginner make some progress.

The cardiovascular system is the heart and the lungs, cardio meaning heart (the pump), vascular meaning veins, arteries and the circulatory system. To increase the efficiency of the cardiovascular system effectively you have to exercise at a rate which causes you to breathe more heavily or elevates the pulse over a period of time – ideally 25 to 30 minutes. This does not mean to say that you have to go into oxygen debt (shortage of breath or gasping for breath). Jogging or steady running is aerobic exercise but sprinting, or hard, sudden movement is anaerobic, the opposite to aerobic. Utilising weights or weight training for that purpose is a very specific way of achieving that particular end.

The simplest way to administer cardiovascular exercise is to tell the client, once far enough advanced, to go through the programme non-stop, resting only when sufficiently out of breath to need to. But, of course, when exercises like bench press, seated leg work, isolated work like tricep movements, twists, side bends and so on are being done then it becomes much harder to get into aerobic condition. It is here that specific exercises can play specific roles in fulfilling that objective.

Unquestionably running, or jogging, is the best single cardiovascular exercise. Circuit training or similar comes next, bike work and so on. But if you particularly want to use weights for that type of training then include in your programme dumb-bell swings, repetition cleans, repetition clean and press, step-ups onto box (with or without weights) and squats (again with or without weights). Space these exercises throughout the programme including a maximum of two or three repetitions depending on the ability, age and requirements of the pupil.

A slightly advanced programme for someone looking for a higher level of cardiovascular ability would look something like this:

Warm-up – bike	5 minutes
	Repetitions
Sit-ups	20
Dumb-bell swings	20
Alternate dumb-bell press	15
Squats	15
Stiff arm pull-over	20
Bent over twists	20
Clean and press	10
Pull-down (Laterals)	10
Crunches (Abdominals)	10
Barbell curls	10

Depending on the level of fitness and experience, this series of exercises could be repeated up to three times. It would be necessary for cardiovascular training, of course, to work each exercise consecutively, going through the whole of the exercises with a minimum amount of rest before starting again with the bike and then repeating.

This type of training is not recommended for body-building.

Golden Rules of Safety

Free weights have been the major cause of accidents in gym areas over the years. These areas must be kept safe and tidy. Look at the gym as a whole. The floor area should at all times be kept clear of loose weights. Unused barbells and dumb-bells should always be replaced on racks. Although this sounds easy and in theory is, in practice it is very hard to administer. Two very important rules should be administered right from the word go.

Golden Rule No 1
Educate the client to replace weights on the racks after each exercise.

The first time you instruct a client emphasise this rule. And then – just as important – watch them do it. That in theory should be enough. In practice, it isn't, you can never leave the area for any length of time.

Golden Rule No 2
Always have the gym 'policed'. This goes a long way towards administering a clean gym. And having a clean gym goes a long way towards having a safe gym.

Golden Rule No 3

Check the equipment – collars, pulleys, anything that adjusts or straps on. Also check boards, carpets, floor covering or bare floors, bench tops or whatever may prove to be a hazard. Remember that if an accident ever happens and it can be proved that it was caused by negligence on your part, then insurance claims can be brought against you.

Golden Rule No 4

Teach the correct techniques – lifting, breathing, advising the beginner not to extend himself in the early stages. You should always be seen to be exercising caution in the early stages.

Golden Rule No 5

Always encourage the client to warm up. Regardless of how much experience someone has, the warm-up is an absolute essential. Some twists, some turns, stretching, abdominal work is ideal. If bikes are available they are excellent. The warm-up is necessary so that when the client starts the programme, he/she is far less prone to pull muscles. Continue this theme by advising the client to start each and every exercise with a lighter weight than his/her maximum weight. In other words progress through the sets increasing until you are using optimum weight.

Golden Rule No 6

Encourage the client to wear suitable clothing. This must be something in which the body can move freely; circulation is important. Tight jeans, buckles which may dig into the flesh, tight clothing of any description are out. The body expands during exercise and needs breathing space. To deprive your system of that essential can cause problems. With regard to shoes, it may look Californian style to walk around bare foot but it is unsafe. Even a small half-kilo disc dropped onto someone's foot, not protected by a gym shoe, will cause bruising at the very least.

Golden Rule No 7

Always screen your client. This is possibly the most important rule of all. There are a number of questions that should always be asked before the instructor programmes the client. These are:

How much exercise are you doing at present?

Do you have any physical disabilities ie slipped discs, cartilage trouble, restrictive movements?

Have you had any operations or are you under the doctor at the present time?

Find out at this stage if the client is involved in any regular sport or exercise. In fact find out as much as you can about his background. You then formulate a programme for him taking his age into account. It is common sense that you do not make out the same schedule for an eighty-year-old man as you do for an eighteen-year-old boy.

Always, always err on the side of caution. Rome wasn't built in a day and the individual's quest for fitness is just the same.

5 Nutrition

Within the overall concept of gym management, it is important that some time be spent on nutritional counselling. One of the ultimate aims in running a gymnasium is to help people achieve greater fitness and health. If these aims are not being met, clients will become dissatisfied, lose interest and certainly not rejoin once their memberships expire – or worse, join another gym. You will not only lose a valuable member but also a source of referrals and business will suffer.

For people to achieve success, whether it be in marathon running, body-building or weight loss, equal emphasis should be given to dietary habits and exercise as both are inextricably linked. The word 'diet' means a particular pattern of eating habits and food consumption, eg low-fat diet, weight-loss diet etc.

Any enquiry into physical performance, whether for the person in the street or the aspiring athlete must start with nutrition for the following reasons:

1 It provides the fuel for all biological work, and
2 It provides the essential elements for the synthesis of new tissue and the repair of existing cells.

The French gourmet, Brillat Savarin, wrote 'Man is only the product of his own digestion'. A cruel dismissal of our mental capabilities, but true in the sense that we are what we eat.

Many thousands of books have been written on the nutritional aspects of health, weight loss and sports performance. It is simply not possible in a chapter to cover all aspects of nutrition as related to the fitness industry. What I plan to do is to provide the essential framework of nutrition for health and hopefully whet your appetite to read and gain knowledge on this fascinating topic.

Across the western world medical concern is rising due to the effects of our present eating habits. This problem is a new one. Never before have human beings had so wide a choice or so regular a supply of good food. Scientific evidence also indicates that nutrition is the main environmental factor *within our control* that affects our health.

Today we are continually being bombarded with advertising and fad diets that promise to make us everything from sexier to slimmer. High protein diets claim to make us stronger and certain foods are claimed to have beneficial or even wonder powers. On the other hand, our diet has become the cause for alarm as we hear that almost everything we eat causes cancer or is in some way 'bad' for our health. With all this conflicting information it is no wonder that most people are totally confused about what to eat.

The problem is one of choice. Today processing, refrigeration, freeze drying and world-wide transport have given the developed world a wide variety of food all-the-year round. Yet this ever richer diet parallels the spread of once rare diseases, hardened arteries, heart attacks and strokes. Coronary heart disease is now the major cause of death in Britain. These diseases are to a very great extent diet related and are avoidable if we choose the correct foods. This ability to choose well from such a wide range of foods is not innate but has to be learnt. Only through increasing people's knowledge and awareness of which foods are good for them will we help them to achieve their potential physically and attain a better quality of life in later years.

Many of the diseases brought about by affluence are associated with the consumption of too much food in general and of certain foods in particular. These will be detailed later in the chapter. However, paradoxically, eating too much food is no guarantee that we receive all the nutrients we need. There is evidence that some groups of people may be suffering 'micronutrient' deficiencies, shortages of one or more of the vitamins and minerals which are essential for growth and metabolism. For the most part these deficiencies are not widespread, although at least 15 per cent of women in Britain are thought to be anaemic (iron deficiency). Some of the blame for these essential nutrient deficiences must rest on the type of diet now common in affluent countries, when a large proportion of our energy is derived from 'empty calories' – foods such as sugar, alcohol and some fats which supply large amounts of calories but none of the vital proteins, vitamins and minerals essential to health.

Nutrition for Health

Recent studies have shown that there is a strong correlation between the food we eat and our health, and in order to avoid the diseases that are associated with bad eating habits we have to modify our diet in the following ways:

1 Reduce our consumption of fat
2 Reduce our consumption of sugar
3 Reduce our consumption of salt
4 Increase our consumption of fibre
5 Increase our consumption of fresh as opposed to processed foods

Let us take each of these in turn and examine the implications to our health and the practical ways we can change in response.

Fat

Present medical evidence shows a strong link between a high fat diet and heart disease and cancer. This is by no means the only link. Other factors such as smoking, high blood pressure, lack of exercise, stress, vitamin and mineral deficiency and excess use of refined sugars, have all been linked to these diseases.

We all eat too much fat. The average person consumes around 42 per cent of their calories as fat. This should be reduced to 30 per cent or less and only 10 per cent should be in the form of saturated or animal fats. As we have become more affluent so we have started to increase the quantity of animal products in our diet. This has brought with it a dramatic jump in the consumption of fat as meat begins to replace cereal products and vegetables, which, in turn, reduces our consumption of fibre and complex carbohydrates.

Fat is not always visible as in butter or around the edges of steak, chops or bacon. It is invisible in dairy products such as milk, cheese and even lean meat when the fat is hidden between the muscle fibres themselves.

Types of Fat

There are several ways in which fats can be classified. One such classification divides them into *saturated* and *unsaturated* fats. These two terms, very familiar in the debate between animal fats and heart disease, refer to the number of hydrogen atoms linked to carbon atoms within the molecular structure. A useful analogy is that of a sponge. Saturated fat is like a sponge that is holding all the water possible. A fat with only one hydrogen atom is termed monounsaturated and fat with two or more is termed polyunsaturated. There is a whole spectrum of such fatty acids ranging from almost totally saturated ones like those in lard to highly unsaturated ones like those in fish oil.

The difference between them is immediately evident. Saturated fats like those of lard or butter are solid at room temperature because they come from warm-blooded animals ie the fat is just liquid at their body temperature. Unsaturated fats come from plants and also from fish. As fish are cold-blooded their body temperature is much lower and their fat naturally remains liquid at a much lower temperature.

However it is wrong to assume that all plant oils are unsaturated as both coconut and palm oil are highly saturated. And as these are the oils most commonly used in fast foods, deep frying etc, beware! Be on your guard if you read 'hydrogenated vegetable oil' on the side of a packet. This means that the manufacturer has played around with it and added hydrogen atoms to a vegetable oil, causing it to become saturated and therefore not good for your health.

Fats and Their Function

Human beings need a small amount of fat to maintain health. This requirement is termed the 'essential fatty acids' and the body cannot manufacture these for itself. They are linoleic acid, linolenic acid and arachidonic acid. However the last two can be manufactured from linoleic acid.

The main sources of this essential fat are whole grains, vegetables and nuts. The polyunsaturated oils of corn and safflower are good sources too.

The functions of fat in our diet can be listed as follows:

1 As a concentrated energy source, particularly valuable in prolonged moderate exercise such as marathon running or triathlons.
2 As a source of the essential fatty acids – necessary for good heatlh.
3 As a carrier for the fat soluble vitamins A, D, E and K.
4 As a protector – the kidneys, for example, are protected from accidental injury by a layer of fat which surrounds them.
5 As an insulator – the subcutaneous fat which lies below the skin protects the body from excessive heat loss. However, this can be detrimental under certain exercise conditions where heat loss is necessary to maintain a steady core temperature.

Cholesterol

Cholesterol is a special kind of fat known as derived fat, one of the few that does not contain fatty acid. It is a natural and important constituent of the body used in building brain tissue and sex hormones. The body is capable of manufacturing as much as we need – about 25g (1oz) a month and there is no need to consume any more from our diet. However we do get more through our intake of saturated animal fats which are our only source of dietary cholesterol.

This becomes a problem because it seems probable that the saturated fats and the extra cholesterol in animal fats interfere in some way with the body's regulation of its own cholesterol supply; too much of it gets into the bloodstream.

Once there it begins to build up and block the arteries. In places a fatty streak develops which ulcerates and finally forms scars that make up an atherosclerotic plaque. Then, characteristically in middle age, a blood clot builds up around one of the plaques, constricting the artery. If this occurs in an artery supplying blood to the heart itself, the heart is starved of oxygen and goes into spasm. At best this results in a damaged heart but recovery for the patient; at worst death.

Practical Ways to Reduce Fat in our Diet
- Eat less visible fat – butter, lard, oils etc, replacing butter with a low-fat spread, and trim all fat from meat before cooking.
- Use less fat in the cooking process – by grilling, baking or steaming rather than frying, and drain away any fat from the meat before adding other ingredients.
- Replace high-fat meats, beef, pork, lamb etc with lower-fat, chicken, turkey or fish and try to eat less meat overall replacing this with more vegetables and pulses (beans, peas, lentils).
- Be aware of the invisible fat in milk, cheese, mayonnaise and eggs using the low-fat alternatives where possible.
- Avoid processed foods, eg sausages, pâtés, beefburgers, pies and pastries.

Sugar

Sugar belongs to the food group known as carbohydrates. Carbohydrates are the most fundamental of all nutrients and are probably the most misunderstood.

In the food chain, carbohydrates exist predominantly in the form of plant food although they are also found in dairy products and marginally in shellfish. A good diet would be one that contained a large amount of plant carbohydrate, thereby providing us with starch, sugar and fibre. However problems arise when we process this plant food and create our own refined carbohydrates, stripping away all the fibre, vitamins and minerals and nutrients in general, leaving 'empty calories', sugar, an energy-producing food with all the goodness removed.

It was sweetness that made sugar a prized commodity. Until recently, sweetness was a rarity in our diet. Just before the turn of the century, Europeans consumed 2kg (4lb) of sugar per head per year. Today we consume a staggering 50kg (110lb) of sugar per person per year.

A direct consequence of this increase in sugar consumption has been the decrease in our consumption of complex carbohydrates in the form of cereals. This has more than halved since the turn of the century from 97 per cent to 40 per cent.

This nutritional shift away from starchy foods, bread, potatoes, rice etc, to sugary foods is of great significance. Some scientists believe that sugar is specifically dangerous in a way that is distinct from most other carbohydrates, being blamed for obesity and the attendant physical and psychological problems that include heart disease, diabetes and tooth decay.

Types of Sugar
Simple Carbohydrates All carbohydrates in our diet are built up from combinations of single molecules of different sugars. Monosaccharides or one molecule sugars contain the simple sugars, glucose, fructose, and galactose. Disaccharides are two monosaccharides combined and the most common are sucrose (table sugar), lactose and maltose.
Complex Carbohydrates Polysaccha-

rides are branched chains of many glucose molecules. Plant polysaccharides are starch and cellulose and animal polysaccharide is glycogen, a glucose polymer and our bodies' stored form of carbohydrate.

The main function of carbohydrate within the body is to provide an energy fuel. Hence the reason why the advertising industry promotes sugary foods as 'energy givers'. However the fact is that we do not need sugar for instant energy. In fact the opposite is true. Our bodies will operate more effectively on natural sugar found in complex carbohydrates. Rather than the food industry adjusting the food by increasing the nutritional value, it has simply manipulated food for its own profit and to the detriment of the population's health.

Hypoglycemia – Low Blood Sugar
When we eat starches and sugars our blood sugar level rises. Eating complex CHO such as cereal, potatoes, bread, vegetables or fruit will allow the blood sugar level to rise at a natural speed. However, when we eat simple carbohydrates such as table sugar (sucrose) or chocolate, where the sugar molecules have already been broken down and our digestion has no work to do, we experience a flood of sugar into our bloodstream. This in turn causes an over-reaction in the pancreas which then releases too much insulin (blood sugar regulating hormone) and the blood sugar is quickly removed, resulting in a low blood sugar level. This triggers the hunger mechanism and we will begin to crave more refined sugar, starting the cycle once again.

Many studies have shown a relationship between high incidence of diabetes and a high sugar intake, which highlights the need for us to satisfy our desire for sweetness with naturally sweet foods such as fruits.

Practical Ways to Reduce Sugar in our Diet
- Omit sugar from tea and coffee. Over 50 per cent of sugar is ingested in this way. I guarantee that on returning to your usual dosage of sugar in drinks after only one week's abstinence you will find the drink too sweet. Try it and see!
- Try to use dried fruits or naturally sweet foods where possible in snacks or in cooking. There are many delicious recipes for cakes where dried fruits are substituted for sugar, providing a wholesome high-fibre alternative to high-sugar, high-fat cakes and biscuits.
- Try wherever possible to reduce the amount of processed food in your diet, choosing fresh fruits and vegetables instead. If you must buy convenience foods, then study the labels carefully. Sugar is hidden under a variety of different names – glucose, dextrose, corn syrup, honey, invert sugar, raw cane sugar – to name but a few.
- Be wary of processed meats, roast ham, garlic sausage etc as almost all will have added sugar, as will savoury foods such as chutneys or ketchups. It pays to read labels.
- Try jams and preserves with reduced or no sugar.

Salt
We need to eat a small amount of salt, ie table salt or sodium chloride, just as we need to consume a small amount of fat for good health. Today we tend to eat too much of both.

Our daily need for salt is in the region of 1–2g and it is required for many important functions within the body. It regulates body fluids, particularly water balance. It is important in the transmission of nerve impulses and for the correct functioning of the heart. It is also important in both carbohydrate and protein metabolism.

The problem arises when we consume too much. Most people easily consume ten times the daily requirement and a high salt intake has been strongly associated with high blood pressure (hypertension) which is a major risk factor in the incidence of heart disease.

High blood pressure is known as the silent killer because the only way to find out if we are suffering from this disease is to have our blood pressure checked, something we do not do regularly enough.

Salting our food is a habit. How many times have you observed someone salting his food copiously, before even tasting it? One way of reducing salt consumption would be to stop salting food whilst cooking, thereby reducing the overall salt intake. However, this problem only accounts for around 25 per cent of our salt intake. By far the greatest consumption of excess salt is ingested through processed foods.

The processing of food, as we have seen, removes fibre, vitamins and minerals, those very items which help to add flavour to our food. Therefore in order to redress the balance and because the food manufacturers know of our liking for salty food, salt is added. Did you know that cornflakes are reputed to contain nearly one thousand times more salt than corn on the cob?

As with sugar, many other names are used to denote the presence of salt in packaged foods. Look out for some of the following: monosodium glutamate, a flavour enhancer much used by the Chinese; sodium bicarbonate, a raising agent; sodium nutrite, a preserving and

curing agent; and sodium benzoate, another preserver.

One important point to remember is that we do not need to add extra salt to our food either in cooking or at the table. Sodium exists naturally in many foods: fruits, vegetables (particularly green veg) and grains. It is a matter of re-educating our palates to enjoy the less salty and more subtle flavour in foods.

Practical Ways to Reduce Salt in our Diet
- Start to eliminate excess from your diet by omitting salt at the cooking stage, thereby allowing people to adjust the seasoning themselves, by tasting their food before adding salt at the table.
- Try to reduce consumption of processed and packaged foods including salty snack foods such as peanuts and crisps. We all realise why pubs provide unlimited salted peanuts free, to make us thirsty so we will drink more.
- Certain meats contain high levels of sodium – bacon, gammon, sausages etc and it is best to avoid these where possible as they also contain large amounts of saturated fat.
- Be adventurous with different flavourings such as lemon juice, herbs, spices or mustard instead of salt.

Fibre

Dietary fibre is not strictly a nutrient as it is not absorbed by the body. It is however a package within which nutrients are contained. Processed foods have much of this fibre removed and with it a large amount of the nourishment. This is why whole natural foods are good for us and processed foods such as white bread and white sugar are not so good.

When wholefood is ingested it travels

through the upper part of the alimentary canal relatively slowly, the binding fibres allowing the nutrients to be released gradually. This is one of the reasons why complex carbohydrates, eg bread and fruit, raise the blood sugar level at a natural speed, while refined carbohydrates, eg soft drinks and chocolate, provoke an insulin response.

Fibre gives bulk to our food and therefore eating wholefoods gives the muscles of the intestines the work they are designed to do. The movement of fibre through the lower alimentary tract is comparatively faster than that through the upper, and it is during this stage that fibre absorbs acids in the large bowel. Without the fibre these acids can become toxic, cause irritation and eventually lead to cancer. Cancer of the colon is the second most prevalent cancer.

One way of checking if you are getting enough fibre is that your faeces should be large, soft and easily evacuated. Constipation will not be a problem for those on a good wholefood diet.

Eating too little fibre in our diet has been linked with obesity, diabetes, heart disease, cancer of the colon, diverticulitis (a painful inflammation of the large colon) and haemorrhoids, the latter being caused by pressure irritation of the lower gut.

Types of Fibre
Five groups of compounds make up fibre. These are cellulose, hemicelluloses, lignins, pectins and gums. They are all found in cereal products, vegetables and fruits and all five compounds should be present if our diet is to be healthy. By eating a wide variety of plant carbohydrates we will ensure a healthy digestive system and consequently a healthy body. Our daily allowance should be in the region of 30g (1oz). However, very few of us actually attain this figure. There are many simple tables on the market now that illustrate the fibre content of various foods and allow us to check if we are eating enough.

Practical Ways to Increase Fibre in our Diet

- These foods are high in fibre: wheat, oats, barley, rice, pulses, lentils, red kidney beans, chick peas and dried beans are a few examples but the list is vast; also nuts and seeds, eg peanuts and sunflower seeds but be careful not to eat too many as these are also high in fat. Fresh fruit and vegetables are also good sources, especially with the skin and peel left on.
- A word of caution – it is important to increase the fibre content of your diet gradually as too much too soon can cause extreme discomfort. It is also important to remember that very little benefit will be achieved by taking fibrefill tablets on top of a highly processed diet. Our diet has to return to a good wholefood base.
- Try to start the day with an unrefined cereal breakfast, muesli or porridge and some fruit. Use wholemeal bread for making toast.
- For main dishes baked potatoes are a good filler and peppers, tomatoes and marrows can be used as 'containers' for meat, fish and rice.
- Use wholemeal pasta and rice. Add it to side salads, with raw vegetables and cooked pulses to make an interesting and tasty change.
- If you take sandwiches to work, fill them with low-fat cheese and dates, or plenty of salad and tuna, which is a healthy move away from cold meats.
- Serve fresh fruit salad as the final course or combine fruit with yogurt

to make 'fools'. I am sure you can think of many more interesting and healthy alternatives to our present highly processed diet of the eighties.

Why not ask your members to bring in their favourite healthy recipes and compile your own gym cookery book. This will provide members with a wealth of ideas to try when they get stuck for something different yet healthy to eat, and will also have the added advantage of creating a good club atmosphere.

It is important that good wholefood be viewed as the nourishing, life-giving substance it is rather than as a poor alternative to the 'goodies' the food manufacturing industry advertises with such force. Explore ways to give life to your life and be adventurous.

6 Anatomy and Physiology

This chapter covers the anatomy, physiology, and basic initial treatment of soft tissue injuries as taught on the National Amateur Bodybuilders Association Courses.

Organisation of Tissues

Different cell types in the body are not mixed haphazardly. Those which are alike are arranged together to form tissues, of which there are four main types.

1 Epithelia tissue lines all internal and external surfaces of the body ie blood vessels, glands.
2 Connective tissue provides the framework, connecting, supporting and packing tissues of the body ie red and white blood cells, tendons, cartilage.
3 Nervous tissue provides the nervous network needed throughout the body, allowing necessary information to be passed from one part of the body to another.
4 Muscular tissue performs all physical functions of the human body. There are three types of muscle present in the human body: skeletal, smooth and cardiac. The one we are most concerned with is skeletal muscle.

Muscle Anatomy

Each muscle has a belly made up of thousands of individual muscle fibres.

These fibres are very small in diameter and range in length from a few millimetres to 50cm (20in) in length. No fibre runs the full length of the muscle, but in appearance the muscle is like the fibres of a thick piece of rope.

Each muscle fibre is made of bundles of longitudinal myofibrils; these in turn are made up of actin and myosin, the part of the muscle concerned with contraction. Along its length the fibre is divided up into different sections which look dark and light under a microscope. A pair of these dark and light sections make up an area called a sarcomere.

At each end of the muscle belly is the tendon which attaches the muscle usually to a bone. Muscle fibres are of two types:

1 Fast twitch — for all-out contractions, ie sprinting and weight lifting.
2 Slow twitch — for contractions over a long period of time, ie endurance exercise.

The ratio of these two types of fibres varies from person to person. With training, this percentage of fast/slow twitch fibres can only be altered by 3 to 4 per cent though this area is at present undergoing further investigation. If a person has a ratio of 80:20 (fast:slow) then obviously his/her sporting potential lies in explosive/dynamic sport.

Each muscle fibre is supplied with a nerve fibre which is necessary to cause muscle fibre stimulation, which in turn will lead to the final product of muscle contraction. The impulses for this to occur come from the brain via the spinal cord.

Muscle has an extremely rich blood supply, with each fibre in close contact with the blood capillaries. This system needs to be very efficient in order to allow certain changes to occur when exercise commences. These will be talked about in much more detail later on.

Muscle Physiology

Muscle Contraction

There are two types of muscle contraction in the body:

1 Isotonic
   This type is used when moving a joint, ie bending the elbow with isotonic contraction of the bicep muscle.
2 Isometric
   This is the type used where muscle tension is maintained.

During muscle contraction, the actin and myosin components slide one over the other. They actually form cross bridges between themselves and so allow this sliding process to occur. Energy is needed for this to happen and this is present in the muscle tissue in the form of ATP (Adenosine Triphosphate), which is a compound formed by the body from the foods we take in. During contraction, the ATP is burnt up and forms what is known as ADP (Adenosine Diphosphate). This happens because the ATP loses one of its phosphate radicals (Tri (3) becomes Di (2)) and so becomes ADP. Once muscle contraction has occurred the cross bridges formed become detached and return to their neutral position. The ATP is then re-formed from the ADP by the use of food substances (glucose, amino acids etc) supplied to the muscle fibre by the

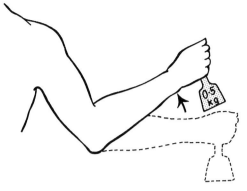

Fig 14 Isotonic muscle contraction

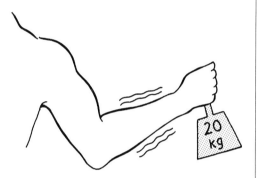

Fig 15 Isometric muscle contraction

extensive network of blood capillaries. Contraction can then re-occur. *Note* For this whole process to occur, Calcium (Ca+) ions need to be present in order to initiate the muscle contraction process.

Recent research seems to show that even the strongest muscle contraction rarely involves a substantial percentage of the total number of muscle fibres present. Also the actual fibre units seem to work in tandem, ie they do not fire all at once but rather one after the other. This adding up of contractions is called summation.

Each muscle fibre has a nerve supply in order to initiate contraction. As well as this stimulatory impulse, there is also an inhibitory impulse which is present most of the time. This prevents the muscle from literally tearing itself apart from the bone.

Muscle Changes During Exercise

During exercise a series of bodily mechanisms are brought into play which result in the working muscles being supplied with more oxygen and essential nutrients, whilst at the same time removing the waste products produced by the working muscle fibres.

When exercise begins, two organs in the body, the pancreas and the adrenal glands produce the hormones glucagen and epinephrine, which mobilise the sugar and fat stores in the body ready for use by the muscles.

The blood vessels in the muscle actually become enlarged and so allow an increased blood flow to the area with an accompanying rise in oxygen. This flow can increase by as much as twenty fold, and this increase in flow is met by the opening of all the muscle capillaries (at rest only 20 per cent are open). With such a dense network of capillaries present the distance which oxygen and other nutrients must pass from capillaries to muscle fibres is greatly reduced. This dilatation occurs because of two factors:

1 Local Regulation
   During muscle activity O_2 (oxygen) concentration falls considerably in the tissue fluids. This in turn causes vasodilatation either because the vessel walls cannot maintain contraction in the absence of O_2 or because O_2 deficiency causes release of some vasodilator material which is thought to be the subtance adenosine.

   Other vasodilator substances released due to muscle contraction include potassium ions, lactic acid, carbon dioxide and ATP. The percentage of each of these substances involved is unknown.

2 Nervous Control
   A network of nerves is present in the body and is called the sympathetic nervous system (SNS). These continually produce impulses, the rate of which can be varied depending on the body's demands, and which have varying effects on certain structures in the body, depending on the number of impulses these receive. The SNS supplies the blood vessels in skeletal muscle and helps to maintain tone in the blood vessel walls.

As the O_2 concentration in the blood begins to fall, as well as affecting the blood vessels, this drop causes signals to be produced in the central mechanisms of the lower brain, which cause the respiratory muscles to work harder and the heart to beat faster with greater strength. The maximum amount of blood pumped by the heart with each beat, called the stroke volume, is soon reached with fairly low levels of exercise. As exercise proceeds there is a decrease in the fluid portion of the blood as this is changed to sweat and transported to the surface of the body. This will cause blood pressure during contraction of the heart (systolic blood pressure) to rise steadily whilst the blood pressure during the resting phase of the heart (diastolic blood pressure) remains fairly constant.

Due to this increase in work within the muscle cells, the muscle temperature will tend to rise. The body then brings certain cooling mechanisms into use – sweating and peripheral blood vasodilatation. In contrast, the blood vessels to the stomach and other abdominal organs actually become narrower in order to allow every available drop of blood to get to the working muscles.

Muscle Fatigue

Prolonged and strong contraction of a muscle causes fatigue to occur. It can be classified as local or general fatigue.

1 Localised fatigue is caused by either a lack of oxygen or nutrients to the working muscle and/or a build-up of muscle waste products such as lactic acid. The nerve impulses still pass to the muscle telling it to contract but the contraction becomes weaker because of the fall in ATP levels.

2 Generalised fatigue depends upon the type of activity undertaken. In all-out activity, eg a 1500m run, fatigue is caused by a build-up of lactic acid as a result of supplying energy primarily by glycalysis. In contrast, fatigue due to a marathon run is primarily caused by factors such as:

(a) prolonged elevation of body temperature (hyperthermia);

(b) depletion of essential nutrients for the muscle;

(c) loss of fluids with consequent adverse fluid/electrolyte balances.

Muscle Hypertrophy

Forceful muscular activity causes the muscle size to increase, leading to hypertrophy: the diameter of each individual muscle fibre increases as well as gaining in various nutrients and important metabolic substances.

For hypertrophy to occur a forceful muscular activity is required even though this activity may only occur for a few moments per day. It is thought that 75 per cent of the muscle must contract for hypertrophy to occur.

Muscle Strength

This is the ability of the muscle or muscle group to apply maximal force with a single contraction. There are several sub-divisions of muscle strength:

1 (a) Isotonic – this is applied through a range of movement to lift a weight, eg biceps curl.

(b) Isometric – this is applied with no movement involved.

2 (a) Concentric – this involves a shortening of the muscle during contraction.

(b) Eccentric – this involves a lengthening of the muscle – 'paying-out'.

The physiological basis of strength is related to several factors. With increased strength, there is an increase in the diameter of the muscle fibres rather than an increase in their number (which is genetically predetermined). It is also related to an ability to suppress some of the inhibiting influences which are constantly supplying the muscle.

In a number of research studies it has been shown that exercises which cause the muscle to contract at near maximal levels for a few repetitions (3–10) are optimal for dynamic strength.

Muscle Endurance

This is the ability of a muscle or group of muscles to work effectively over a long period of time. This is determined mainly by the hereditary factor on the number of fast/slow twitch fibres present. It also involves the efficiency of circulation, in order to transport nutrients to the working muscle and to deal with the resulting lactic acid produced.

Muscle Flexibility

This is the range of possible movement around a joint or sequence of joints. It is dependent on several factors:

1 Alignment of bones.
2 Degree of ligament stretch.

3 Amount of muscle/fat/soft tissue.

Genetics again have a great bearing on this although most athletes are capable of improved flexibility. Flexibility training is of two types, passive static stretches at a joint and active associated movements. This is a very neglected area of rehabilitation following injury and often leads to chronic injury problems.

The concept that weight training causes reduced flexibility is only true when the training does not involve a full range of movements in the joints concerned. In fact, if progressive training is done through the full range, flexibility is often improved!

It should be emphasised that warm-up before exercise has been shown to improve the flexibility in a given joint.

Muscle Cramp

This is a type of local spasm in the muscle. It can be caused by several factors, severe cold, lack of blood or fatigue. This produces a painful response via the spinal cord and increases contraction. As contraction increases so pain stimulation increases leading to a vicious circle until muscle cramp occurs.

Joint Anatomy

A joint is a junction between two bone ends. The majority of joints allow movement, but some are shaped so as to interlock and block motion eg sacrum/coccyx. The major joints that come under stress with regard to weight training are the following:

Shoulder-joint

This is classed as a ball and socket joint, due to its wide range of movement. The bones involved are the head (ball) of the humerus, and the glenoid cavity (socket) of the scapula (shoulder-blade).

The actual socket part of the shoulder joint is very shallow, and so actually provides very little support when a traction force is applied to the shoulder-joint. Structurally, therefore, the joint is very weak, and so is very dependent on the support given by surrounding muscles and ligaments. Dislocation is very common.

The major muscles which affect the shoulder-joint are:

1 Deltoid
   This consists of three groups of fibres, anterior, intermediate and posterior. These groups originate from the clavicle (collar bone) and scapula (shoulder-blade), and at their insertion they form a tendon which attaches to the upper/outer part of the humerus.
2 Pectoralis Major
   This is a triangular-shaped muscle which originates from the clavicle and sternum (chest bone) and inserts into the upper part of the humerus.
3 Biceps
   This has two origins, from different parts of the scapula, it then passes over the front of the humerus to attach to the upper end of the radius, one of the two bones in the forearm. This muscle, because it works over two joints (the shoulder and the elbow) is very often injured. This also applies to other muscles in the body which anatomically have the same function eg quadriceps and hamstrings (see hip- and knee-joint).
4 Rotator Cuff Muscles
   This group consists of four smaller muscles: subscapularis, supra-spinatous; teres minor and infraspinatous. These have an essential job in preventing

81

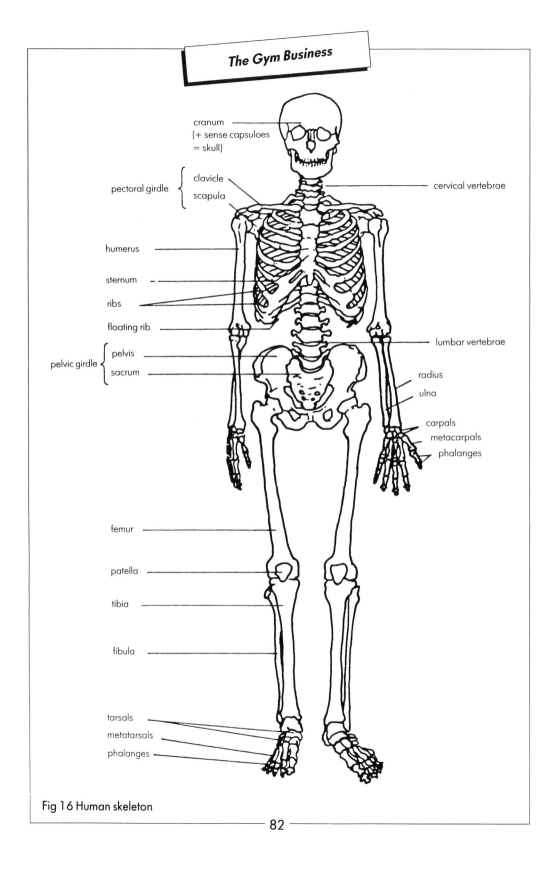

cranum
(+ sense capsuloes
= skull)

cervical vertebrae

pectoral girdle {
clavicle

scapula

humerus

sternum

ribs

floating rib

lumbar vertebrae

pelvic girdle {
pelvis

sacrum

radius

ulna

carpals

metacarpals

phalanges

femur

patella

tibia

fibula

tarsals

metatarsals

phalanges

Fig 16 Human skeleton

dislocation, when the arm is hanging by the side.

The Neck and Back

The spine/vertebral column includes two main areas where injuries are likely to occur when weight training, the neck and back. The spine consists of a column of bony vertebrae, with discs made of cartilage separating them. These structures are supported by ligaments and muscles which allow only certain movements – flexion, extension, side flexion and rotation (to the left and right). Each vertebra interconnects with the one above and below via small joints and so allows restricted movements to take place. The range of movement varies between individuals, but is thought to be mostly inherited. Running through the whole length of the spinal column is the spinal cord from which emanate the nerves supplying the rest of the body.

The major muscles which affect the neck and back are:

1   Trapezius
    This muscle covers the back of the neck and upper spine. It originates from the top of the skull and the upper half of the vertebral column attaching to the clavicle and scapula on either side.
2   Latissimus Dorsi
    Extends from the lumbar region and lower thoracic spine, inserting into the humerus by a tendon approximately 7cm (2¾in) long.
3   Erector Spinae
    Originates from the sacrum (lower end of the spinal column) covering the lumbar and lower thoracic vertebrae on either side.

The Hip-joint

This joint, like the knee and ankle can easily be injured when a load is put through the skeleton. It is very similar in classification to the shoulder, being a ball and socket joint, the head of the femur (thigh-bone) articulating with the cup-shaped cavity of the pelvis. The actual socket part of the joint though is much deeper than that of the shoulder socket, so giving a better joint alignment. The dependence therefore on ligament/muscle support in order to prevent dislocation, is much less than that of the shoulder, though still very necessary.

The major muscles which affect this joint are:

1   Psoas
    Originates from the lateral (outer) aspect of the lumbar vertebrae, and attaches to the upper outer aspect of the femur.
2   Iliacos
    These muscle fibres originate from the pelvic and sacral bone, and join the tendon of the psoas to attach to a similar part of the femur as above.
3   Quadriceps
    Made up of four muscles: Rectus Femoris; Vastus Medialis; Lateralis; Intermedius. These muscles cover the anterior aspect of the femur originating from the pelvis and upper part of the femur to pass over the patella (kneecap) to attach into the upper, anterior aspect of the tibia. This muscle, therefore, works over two joints, hip and knee, increasing its chances of injury.
4   Hamstrings
    Made up of three muscles: Semimembranosis; Semitendonosis; Biceps Femoris. This group covers the posterior aspect of the thigh, originating from the lower part of the pelvic-bone and inserting into the posterior aspects of the tibia and fibula (shin-bones). This muscle again belongs to the two-joint

muscle group.

5 Gluteii

Made of three muscles: Gluteus Maximus; Medius; Minimus. These muscles cover the buttock region of the lower limb, originating from the pelvic-bone and attaching to the upper, posterior aspect of the femur.

The Knee-joint

This joint is classed as a condylar joint due to its limitation of movement in one plane ie flexion and extension. The articulating surfaces are the lower end of the femur, upper end of the tibia, and posterior surface of the patella. It is well supported externally and internally by ligamentous structures, and is also very dependent on the support given by the surrounding musculature.

The major muscles which affect this joint are quadriceps and hamstrings (see hip-joint).

Acute Soft-Tissue Injuries

This type of injury includes damage to muscles, tendons, ligaments and joint capsule and may occur either on their own or with fracture/dislocation.

This damage often occurs in these areas when no medical advice may be available, so some basic treatment will go a long way, particularly in the first forty-eight hours when half the battle can be won or lost.

When a muscle/tendon/ligament tears, not only do the fibrous structures tear but also the blood capillaries around those fibres. This causes internal bleeding, which can take up to forty-eight hours to cease. Once this has stopped, the damaged area is replaced by what is called scar tissue, a very inflexible structure, which needs to be broken down before normal muscle

tissue can re-form. It is very important that this tissue forms in order to allow good muscle tissue to reappear.

Once an injury of this type occurs, the most important factors are:

1 Rest

It takes a minimum of twenty-one days for muscle tissue, forty-two days for ligaments/tendons to repair fully. Initial, strict rest is necessary in order to allow this clotting process to occur.

2 Ice

Not heat, which can cause increased tissue damage if applied within the first forty-eight hours. Ice packs, frozen peas, cold compress, chemical packs, etc are all forms of ice therapy available. These can be applied every two hours, for fifteen minutes at a time to gain maximum benefit.

3 Compression

To reduce the amount of swelling use wool and crêpe bandaging which can be altered should excessive swelling occur after the injury.

4 Elevation

Keep the injured part raised to help return excess fluid back to the heart.

These basic rules can be remembered by the first letter of each word, so forming RICE.

Once the first forty-eight hours is over, then heat treatment and stretching exercises are very useful forms of rehabilitation. At this stage though, you as an instructor have performed the basic treatment. Any further problems should then be passed on to the medical profession, a GP, consultant or physiotherapist depending on the degree of injury.

Sports Injuries Checklist

- **S**trapping – used to immobilise a joint or to give support. Tubigrip only prevents swelling and gives only psychological support
- **P**hysiotheraphy – a complete rehabilitation treatment for the injured sportsman/women. Qualified physiotherapists hold the letters MCSP SRP
- **O**ther sports – very useful when an athlete is unable to compete in his own sport
- **R**est – the most important treatment for injuries, yet the most ignored
- **T**emperature – heat over an injured area means an inflammatory process is going on and treatment is required
- **S**welling – a second factor seen and felt when a soft-tissue injury occurs
- **I**ce – the first treatment to be applied to an immediate injury
- **N**ever forget – pain is a warning that something is wrong, and should never be ignored
- **J**udgement – necessary to allow the injured athlete to return to full training
- **U**nderstand – the injured, who is often a very frustrated athlete
- **R**edness – the third factor seen in the inflammatory process
- **I**nfra-red – and other forms of heat applied to an injury 48–72 hours after the moment of trauma
- **E**levation – of an immediate injury prevents the build-up of swelling, along with compression of the injured part
- **S**tretching – very necessary after a muscle tear to prevent a recurrent, chronic injury from arising

7 Future Trends

In the thirty-seven years that I have been involved in the fitness industry there have been many changes. The once predominant and insular physical culture is now a more sophisticated and varied industry marketing to every section of the public. Certainly at the present time keeping pace with the changes and anticipating the direction in which they will go is a problem — though I might add, a good and challenging one.

Twenty years ago we set up in business with a few weights and even fewer machines, ready then as now to respond to whatever the market place dictated. The installation of our first sauna had immediate appeal to our public. Three years later we installed a glittering array of chrome equipment, wall-to-wall carpets (when 5×4 and 4×3 were popular) and piped background music. That transformed the back-street gym with sawdust on the floor and spitoons to a luxurious and sophisticated, desirable place to work out.

When squash was thought of only as a drink we installed our first court and invited the legendary Jonah Barrington to give a clinic. The boom was set to come and we had gambled right again. The decision to equip with a spa bath preceded the household word jacuzzi and aerobics were confused with aerobatics. When we were first on the scene with dance-orientated fitness classes I originated a cassette-tape male version of aerobics called 'Fitness' which in turn developed into 'Fatigues'. At one stage and for a number of years we had five hundred men a week doing the classes. Recognising a gap in the market

and a need to fill it resulted in our survival in an over-populated and highly competitive industry.

The swing in popularity was going towards the gym areas again and the developments in technology worldwide were having an impact on the industry. Computerised machines with goal-setting displays were coming to the fore and although weight-resisted and cam-operated machines would be around for some time it was clear that the computer would take over from the selectorised-type machine.

Ringing the changes can be a dicey occupation and you must realise that even the good moves are not necessarily immediately profitable. The service industry of which we are part relies heavily on image and the moves are very often of a tactical nature to confuse the opposition and to create interest among your clients and the prospective customer.

Responding to change means not lagging behind the competitors all round you. Staying ahead is first recognising change and then having the courage to respond. When things are going well it is a difficult decision to make. I have often thought, why should I change? The answer is, if you do not change with the times your competitors will and you will be left far behind.

I would still like to see our industry grow to acceptance on a level with other professions. This would involve both the progressive and established schools of excellence with opportunities for people to qualify in the skills of management and business procedure. I would hope that

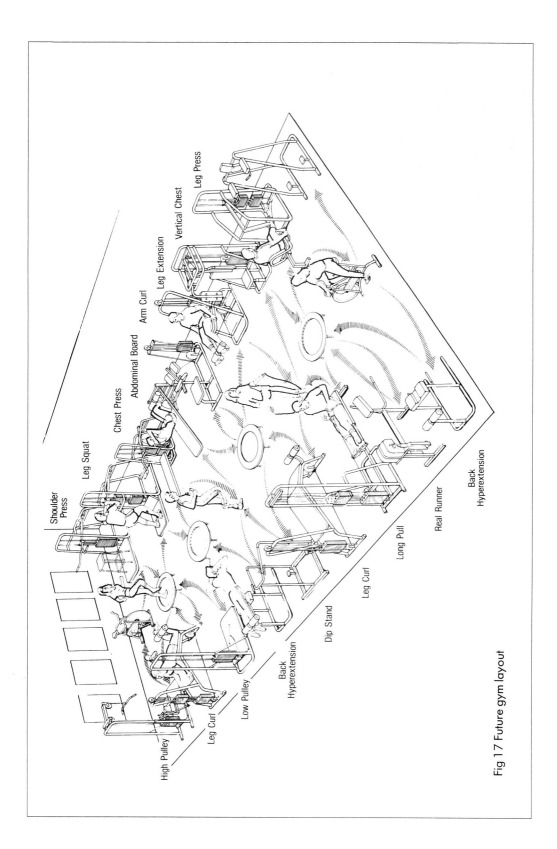

Fig 17 Future gym layout

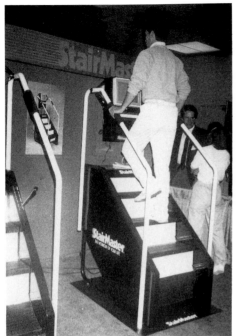

our efforts to promote the NABBA Insrtuctors' Courses and our business seminars have been seen as a genuine effort to gain a credibility that has been sadly lacking over the last twenty years. I also hope that other people will take encouragement from our success by setting their sights on improving our profession. I can see the European market outstripping the American market and certainly the potential growth of the professional gym business in Europe is unlimited.

There is little doubt that we are entrenched in the machine age with both electronic and manual equipment. The machines will continue to become more

Nobody likes climbing stairs, but everyone wants to use the StairMaster

A hint of things to come

The latest trends

and more sophisticated aesthetically, relying more and more on computer-based feedback. However, do not rule out man's instincts to lift and pitch his strength against heavy objects – free weights – that will be with us for years.

The percentage of people attracted to our facilities will increase due to a larger proportion of leisure time and the improvements in our industry, and there might easily be a soaring of preventative medicine with government legislation promoting it.

Governments have for years evaded their responsibilities in promoting health and fitness on a large scale. The use of grants to promote medically approved fitness centres has also been sadly lacking. The private health sector has given little direction regarding exercise as it has become more and more sophisticated. It tells you what is wrong but fails to prescribe sufficient after-care service or advice on prevention.

The seeds for the future need to be planted in the minds of our children. Perhaps then politicians, health centres, the medical profession and the public at large will have a common ground to work from. One can only hope that this will happen.

As we move into the twenty-first century and the new age, the health and fitness industry will undoubtedly gain in stature. Controllable, monitored, interesting exercise will appeal to a broader section of the public and we will see more and more older people utilising the gyms, not just as a means to an end but also as a social outlet.

The gym business will have to compete in the future just as the High Street shops are competing now and many will go under just as in any other aspect of life. Undoubtedly, the strong will survive.

Regardless of the development of our industry technologically or otherwise the challenge for the future will come through people, for we are in the people business.

Appendices

Further Reading

Gray's Anatomy (35th edition)

de Bono, Edward; *Tactics, The Art and Science of Success*

Iacocca, Lee; *Iacocca, An Autobiography*

Pearl, Bill; *Getting Stronger*

Pearl, Bill; *Keys to the Inner Universe* (two excellent books for the gym instructor)

Peterson & Renstrom, *Sports Injuries*

Peterson & Renstrom, *Sports Medicine*

Sperryn, Peter, *Sport and Medicine*

Sutherland, David & Sheperdson, Harold, *Football Injuries and Fitness*

Acknowledgements

I personally feel a deep obligation to an industry that has provided a living both to myself and the people around me. If I can serve this industry and hopefully help its progression, raise its credibility and professionalism, then I will have the satisfaction not only of doing the job I know I do well but also of putting back into the industry some of the knowledge I have gained over the years. I would like to mention some of the people who have been an inspiration to me.

The lessons we learn in business are not always appropriate to the business that we are in. The lessons I learnt from Joe Moss – the 'Umbrella Man' who marketed umbrellas in winter and suitcases in summer, identifying the market needs – stick in my mind year after year after year. The half hour I spent on the squash court with Jonah Barrington – not a lesson in squash but a lesson in basics – taught me that just hitting the ball up and down side walls and practising what you want to do well is as important in business as it is on the squash court.

Bill Pearl's statement that, each and every day, he had to motivate himself to get out there and do it applied both to body-building and to business.

A good friend of mine, Michael Smyth, who sells cars and petrol in a very professional manner, has taught me more about standards than I could ever have learned by studying the gym business.

My thanks go to the various equipment manufacturers – David, Force Equipment, Sports Engineering, Life Systems, Universal Gym Company, Nautilus – who have been kind enough to spend time and effort in providing me with the relevant photographs and information.

Special thanks also to my partner, Bill Stevenson, for his undying loyalty over the last thirty-five years. Also to Hank Howlett, Michael Phipps of the Nautilus Gym in Pontefract, Tony Armstrong and Eddie Renshaw. To Karan Thomas, BSc Hons, Phys Ed, Nutritionist, for the chapter on nutrition and to David Fevre, Senior Orthopaedic Physiotherapist, MCSP, SRP for the chapter on anatomy and physiology; and to the team we call our staff. And, of course, David & Charles.

And finally to Holly Bonfield without whose constant energy and advice this book would never have seen completion.

Manufacturers and Suppliers

United Kingdom

Equipment

Association of Play Industries,
Prudential House,
10th Floor, Wellesley Road,
Croydon, Surrey CR0 9XY
Tel: 01 681 1242

Atlanta Sports Industries,
Atlanta House,
Rotherway, Crowley Ind Est,
Maltby,
Rotherham SG6 8QN
Tel: 0709 700555

Avon Gymnasium
Manufacturing Co Ltd,
12 Coombend, Radstock,
Bath, Avon BA3 3AN
Tel: 0761 37313

Bolton Stirland Int Ltd,
Boland House,
Nottingham South Ind Est,
Ruddington Lane, Wilford,
Nottingham NG11 7EP
Tel: 0602 822844

Compactagym Ltd,
Royal London House,
28/31 St Mary St,
Cardiff CF1 2AB
Tel: 0222 371039

Competition Line (UK) Ltd,
Unit 6, Sky Business Centre,
Eversley Way, Thorpe,
Egham, Surrey TW20 8RF
Tel: 0784 71466

Diversified Products Ltd,
Phoenix Way, Garngoch Ind Est,
Gorseinon, Swansea SA4 1WF
Tel: 0792 894891

Force Equipment Ltd,
Drakes Industrial Estate,
Egerton,
Bolton
Tel: 0204 593829

Gym Build,
Unit 8/10, Campbell St Ind Est,
Campbell St,
Preston
Tel: 0772 795666

Gym 80,
36 Woodman Rd,
Brentwood,
Essex CM14 5BE
Tel: 0277 262750

Gympac Systems Ltd,
Unit 5, Ty Verlon Ind Est,
Cardiff Rd, Barry,
S Glamorgan CF6 3BE
Tel: 0446 737094/742145

Gymplex UK Ltd,
36 Woodman Rd, Brentwood,
Essex CM14 5BE
Tel: 0277 262750

Hydra Fitness (Europe) Ltd,
Unit 25, Hortonwood 33,
Telford, Shropshire TF1 4ES
Tel: 0952 608442/608137

Life Fitness Systems Ltd,
Stanley House, Victoria St,
Littleport, Ely,
Cambs CB6 1LZ
Tel: 0353 860089

Livingwell Health & Leisure,
7 Old Park Lane,
London, W1
Tel: 01 493 0105

Minotaur Sports Eng Ltd,
Unit 1, Battle Road,
Heathfield Ind Est,
Newton Abbot,
South Devon
Tel: 0626 832245

Nautilus UK,
Woodberry House,
Woodberry Down,
Epping, Essex CM16 6RJ
Tel: 0378 560120

Nissan/Universal,
33 Tallon Road,
Brentwood, Essex CM13 1TT
Tel: 0277 221122

Peak Fitness,
Unit 29, Cutlers Rd,
Saltcoats Ind Estate,
South Woodham Ferrers,
Chelmsford, Essex CM3 5XJ
Tel: 0245 324222

Polaris International,
Norman House, Heritage Gate,
Derby DE1 1NU
Tel: 0332 381853

Powersport International Ltd,
Queens Road, Bridgend Ind Est,
Bridgend, Glamorgan,
South Wales CF31 3DE
Tel: 0656 61164

Precor Europe,
Drummond House,
94 Broad Street,
Birmingham B15 1AU
Tel: 021 631 2373

Pulse Star Gym Systems,
Units 4 & 5, Varey Road,
Eaton Bank Trading Estate,
Congleton,
Cheshire CW12 1UW
Tel: 0260 280359

Raven Physique,
806 High Rd,
Tottenham,
London N17
Tel: 01 801 7402

J. Schnell (UK) Ltd,
250 Durnsford Rd,
London SW19 8DS
Tel: 01 946 0502

Sport Engineering Ltd,
Stirchley Trading Estate,
Hazelwell Road,
Birmingham B30 2PF
Tel: 021 459 8193/8383

Sportesse (UK) Ltd,
61–63 High St, Aylesbury,
Bucks HP20 1SA
Tel: 0296 29730

Sports & Leisure Marketing Ltd,
Unit 2, New Inn Bridge Estate,
998 Foleshill Road,
Coventry CV6 6NE
Tel: 0203 637763

Taurus Treadmills,
Charingworth Grange,
Charingworth,
Chipping Campden,
Glos GL55 6XY
Tel: 038678 438

Tay Sport & Fitness Ltd,
Unit 2, Whitworth Ind Park,
Tilton Rd,
Birmingham B9 4PP
Tel: 021 771 4590

Terry of Redditch Ltd,
Millsbro Road, Redditch,
Worcs B98 7AH
Tel: 0527 64261

Sunbeds
Helionova Limited,
38 Morgan Way,
Bowthorpe Employment Area,
Norwich NR5 9JJ
Tel: 0603 748061

Jomi UK Ltd,
41 Briggate,
Shipley,
West Yorks BD17 7BP
Tel: 0274 599428

Leisure Marketing,
27 Trevarrick Court,
Horwich,
Bolton BL6 6TF
Tel: 0204 693981

Solana Industries Ltd,
4 Halifax Road,
Greenford,
Middx UB6 8XU
Tel: 01 575 8525

Ultratan International Ltd,
Ultratan House,
Star Road, Hillingdon,
Middx UB10 0QL
Tel: 01 756 0118

Uvalight Leisure,
9th Floor, St Martins House,
10 The Bull Ring,
Birmingham B5 5DT
Tel: 021 643 2463/2472

Saunas
Dalesauna Ltd,
8 East Parade,
Harrogate,
N. Yorks HG1 5LT
Tel: 0423 522241

Suntrap Systems Ltd,
105 Argent Centre,
Frederick Street,
Birmingham B1 3HS
Tel: 021 236 2642

Swedish Saunas Limited,
11 Baneswell Rd,
Newport, Gwent NP9 4BP
Tel: 0633 56442

Miscellaneous
Dex-O-Tex Sports Surfaces,
15 Blenheim Road,
Cressex Ind Est,
High Wycombe,
Bucks HP12 3RS
Tel: 0494 36282

Helmsman Coin Controlled
Lockers Ltd,
Northern Way,
Bury St Edmunds,
Suffolk IP32 6NH
Tel: 0284 752812

Microcache Computer
Consultants,
Stand No 31,
17 The Forty,
Cholsey,
Oxfordshire OX10 9NA
Tel: 0491 652121

Premier Lockers Ltd,
Church Rd, Catshill,
Bromsgrove, Worcs B61 0JY
Tel: 0527 72536

Prospec International Ltd,
PO Box 48,
Canklow Meadows Est,
West Bawtry Rd,
Rotherham S60 2XP
Tel: 0709 377147

Sargent & Potiriadis,
Architects & Leisure Planners,
S & P House,
3–5 Charing Cross Rd,
London WC2H 0HA
Tel: 01 930 9010

Slim Gym Limited,
Whaley Bridge,
Stockport SK12 7LY
Tel: 06633 4545

Sports Industry,
PO Box 13,
Hereford House,
Bridle Path,
Croydon CR9 4NL
Tel: 01 680 4200

Sport & Leisure Magazine,
Sports Council,
16 Upper Woburn Place,
London WC1H 0QP
Tel: 01 388 1277

The Body Programme,
Leyland Health and Fitness
Centre,
Eden Street,
Leyland, Lancashire
Tel: 0772 45161

Universal Computers Ltd,
23 Paradise St,
London SE16 4QD
Tel: 01 232 1155

United States of America
Equipment
Magnum II
by Badger Fitness Equipment,
1010 Davis Avenue,
South Milwaukee,
Wisconsin 53172

Bodyguard by Oglaend,
40 Radio Circle,
Mount Kisco, New York 10549

Body Masters Sports
Industry Inc,
700 East Texas Avenue,
PO Box 259,
Rayne, Louisiana 70578

California Gym Equipment,
3140 East Pico Boulevard,
Los Angeles, California 90023

Challenger Fitness
Equipment Inc,
8201 Sovereign Row,
Dallas, Texas 75247

David Fitness Equipment Inc,
Carriage IV Building,
1086 Teaneck Road,
Teaneck, New Jersey 07666

Diversified Health Club
Services Inc,
42 Aero Camino, Suite 214,
Goleta, California 93117

Eagle Fitness Systems By Cybex,
2100 Smithtown Avenue,
Ronkonkoma, New York 11779

First Equipment Leasing
Corporation,
7601 North Federal Highway,
Boca Raton, Florida 33431

First Fitness Equipment
International,
PO Box 330117,
Fort Worth, Texas 76163

Hoggan Health Industries Inc,
111 East 12300 South,
Draper, Utah 84020

James Design Company,
5116 East Chestnut Avenue,
Vineland, New Jersey 083600

Kidcycle By Apparent Inc,
13348 Grass Valley Avenue,
Grass Valley, California 95945

Keiser Sports Health Equipment,
411 South West Avenue,
Fresno, California 93706

Kozy Inc,
3712 North Halsted,
Chicago, Illinois 60613

Life Fitness,
9601 Jeronimo Road,
Irvine, California 92718

Nautilus Sports/Medical
Industries Inc,
Drawer 809014,
Dallas, Texas 75380

Pacer Industries Inc,
1121 Crowley,
Carrolton, Texas 75006

Paramount Fitness Equipment
Corporation,
6450 East Bandini Boulevard,
Los Angeles, California 90040

Patex International Inc,
1 South "A" Street, Suite 204,
Pensacola, Florida 32501

Polaris by Iron Co,
PO Box 1458,
Spring Valley,
California 92077

Powercise International,
111 North Post Oak Lane,
Houston, Texas 77024

Precor USA,
PO Box 3004,
Bothel, Washington 98041

Pyramid Fitness Industries,
854 South Irvine Avenue,
Masury, Ohio 44438

Quinton Instrument Company,
An A. H. Robins Company,
3800 Cutshaw Avenue,
Richmond, Virginia 23230

Sta-Fit Gym Equipment,
110 North College Avenue,
Aledo, Illinois 61231

Stairmaster Sports/Medical
Products,
259 Route 17K,
Newburgh, New York 12550

Stairobic,
670 North Commercial Street,
Manchester,
New Hampshire 03101

T.K. Gym Equipment,
6 Franklin Avenue,
Mount Vernon, New York 10550

Trotter Inc,
1073 Main Street,
Millis, Massachusetts 02054

Unisen Inc, Startrack,
14352 Chambers Road,
Tustin, California 92680

Universal Gym Equipment Inc,
930 27th Avenue SW,
PO Box 1270,
Cedar Rapids, Iowa 52406

York Barbell Company Inc,
PO Box 1707,
York, Pennsylvania 17405

National Amateur Bodybuilders Association

The National Amateur Bodybuilders Association is the longest established organisation of its kind in existence. Recognised throughout the bodybuilding world, NABBA has led the way in physique and figure competition for nearly four decades. The driving force behind NABBA for most of those thirty odd years has been Oscar Heidenstam, who until recent years has organised almost single-handedly the Mr Universe Amateur and Professional and also the Mr Britain competitions. The world's best physiques have graced the podiums of The London Palladium, the Victoria and New Victoria Palaces, La Scala and many more theatres in capital cities.

Arnold Schwarzenegger, John Grimek, Bill Pearl, Reg Park, Steve Reeves – legends of today and of the past – have fiercely competed for the coveted crowns of the supreme title in the world under the auspices of NABBA.

NABBA has been predominant in organising also the Scottish, Welsh and Irish competitions and area competitions throughout the British Isles. At one stage twenty-three countries were organising competitions under the banner of NABBA.

Ken Heathcote became a member of NABBA in 1953 and competed in competitions for over fifteen years. He became a senior judge and has officiated and judged at every level – local, national and international including the Mr Universe.

The formulation of the NABBA Instructors and Senior Instructors Weight Training Courses was directly due to Ken Heathcote and Oscar Heidenstam's agreement that a level of competent instruction was much needed in raising the credibility of the industry. Ken Heathcote then took the step forward by organising and formulating a programme, both practical and theoretical, to meet the needs of a growing industry that now reaches into every level of our social strata. Hard-core bodybuilding, still the purest expression, is however only part of a much wider concept, and weight training and the gym business are now coming of age.

NABBA's endorsement of the formulation of the courses has undoubtedly brought bodybuilding into the twentieth century.

Index

Accounts 11
Additional income 45
Advertising 10, 30, 33–36
Aerobic classes 18, 58–59
   age 59
   beginners 59
   content 59
   cool-down 59
   music 59
   warm-up 58–59
America 10, 20

Bodybuilding 21, 22, 28
   gyms 22, 26–29

Capital 11–12
Changing area 18
Cholesterol 71–72
Cleaning 10

Dance teaching 58

Equipment 12, 22–27
   aerobic 16–17, 22, 24–26, 66, 68
   cam operated 22

Fat 70–72
   cholesterol 71–72
   function of 71
   types of 70–71
Fatigues 57
Fibre 74–76
   types of 75
   ways to increase in diet 75–76
Fitness assessment 59–61
Fitness centre 22
Free weights 22–23, 27, 87
Front desk 50

Group classes 56–57
Guest pass card 44–45
Gym, types of 20–22

Hygiene 54
Hypoglycemia 73

Iacocca, Lee 11

Image 31–32, 47
Injuries, acute soft tissue 84
   checklist 85
Insurance 19–20

Joints 81
   hip 83–84
   knee 84
   neck and back 83
   shoulder 81–83

Launch 29–30
Layouts 15–17, 24, 87
Leaflet drop 43
Location 12–14
Lockers 18

Machines 27
Maildrop 43
Management 47–48
Market, identification of 32
Membership, maintenance of 45–46
   turnover 41
Membership fees 13, 29, 40, 42, 44
Mixed training 20
Muscle anatomy 77–78
Muscle physiology 78
   changes during exercise 79
   contraction 78–79
   cramp 81
   endurance 80
   fatigue 80
   flexibility 80–81
   hypertrophy 80
   strength 80

NABBA 49, 94

Open day 36, 41–44
Opening hours 9, 55

Payments, types of 40, 44
Pearl, Bill 9
Personal invitation 43
Personal relations 45–46
Plumbing 17–18
Premises 14–16

Pricing 29
Programmes, formulation of 62–67
Promotions 44–45
Profit 9–10, 45–46

Raising capital 11
Reception 18
Records 50–53
Reinvestment 12

Safety 20, 22, 67–68
Salt 73
Sandow, Eugene 28
Saunas 10, 12

Security 54–55
Selling 31, 36–41, 46
Selling tour 38–40
Staff 48–50
Standards 12, 48, 52, 54
Sugar 72
    types of 72
    ways to reduce in diet 73
Sunbeds 26, 44
Sweeney, Bob 7–8
Swimming pool 20–21, 26

Tissues, organisation of 77
Total body workout 61